Lecture Notes in Computer Science   11086

Commenced Publication in 1973
Founding and Former Series Editors:
Gerhard Goos, Juris Hartmanis, and Jan van Leeuwen

More information about this series at http://www.springer.com/series/7410

George Cybenko · David Pym ·
Barbara Fila (Eds.)

Graphical Models
for Security

5th International Workshop, GraMSec 2018
Oxford, UK, July 8, 2018
Revised Selected Papers

 Springer

Editors
George Cybenko ⓘD
Dartmouth College
Hanover, NH, USA

David Pym ⓘD
University College London
London, UK

Barbara Fila ⓘD
IRISA, INSA Rennes
Rennes, France

ISSN 0302-9743   ISSN 1611-3349   (electronic)
Lecture Notes in Computer Science
ISBN 978-3-030-15464-6   ISBN 978-3-030-15465-3   (eBook)
https://doi.org/10.1007/978-3-030-15465-3

Library of Congress Control Number: 2019933891

LNCS Sublibrary: SL4 – Security and Cryptology

This Springer imprint is published by the registered company Springer Nature Switzerland AG
The registered company address is: Gewerbestrasse 11, 6330 Cham, Switzerland

Preface

The 5th International Workshop on Graphical Models for Security (GraMSec) was held at Oxford, UK, on July 8, 2018, in conjunction with the Federated Logic Conference (FLoC) 2018.

Previous GraMSec workshops were held in Grenoble, France (2014), Verona, Italy (2015), Lisbon, Portugal (2016), and Santa Barbara, USA (2017). GraMSec 2019 will be held at Hoboken, USA on June 24, 2019, co-located with the 32nd IEEE Computer Security Foundations Symposium.

GraMSec workshops bring together international researchers interested in the use of graphical security models to represent and analyze the security of systems. This topic has gained considerable research attention over the past two decades, and the workshop allows the community of security researchers, as well as security professionals from industry and government, to exchange ideas and advances in graphical security models, metrics, and measurements. Such graphical models are being used to capture different security facets and can address a range of challenges including security assessment, automated defence, secure services composition, security policy validation, and verification.

Specific technical areas addressed by the GraMSec workshops include:

– Graph representations: mathematical, conceptual, and implemented tools for describing and reasoning about security
– Logical approaches: formal logical tools for representing and reasoning about graphs and their use as modeling tools in security
– Machine learning: modeling and reasoning about the role of big data and machine learning in security operations
– Networks in national security: terrorist networks, counter-terrorism networks; safety in national infrastructure (e.g., utilities and transportation)
– Risk analysis and management: models of risk management in business and organizational architectures
– Social networks: using and reasoning about social graphs, network analysis, network protocols, social mapping, sociometry

These proceedings consist of the seven accepted papers, which were selected from 21 submissions. In addition to presentations based on these papers, Michael Fisk of Los Alamos National Laboratory gave a keynote talk titled "Intrusion Tolerance in Complex Cyber System".

Graphical security models provide powerful mechanisms for modern complex systems security expression and analysis. These proceedings illustrate that the technical area is broad and advancing in several novel and exciting directions.

February 2019

George Cybenko
David Pym
Barbara Fila

Organization

Program Committee

Ludovic Apvrille	Telecom ParisTech, France
Stefano Bistarelli	Università di Perugia, Italy
Tristan Caulfield	University College London, UK
Nora Cuppens-Boulahia	IMT Atlantique, France
George Cybenko	Dartmouth College, USA
Harley Eades III	Augusta University, USA
Barbara Fila	INSA Rennes, IRISA, France
Olga Gadyatskaya	SnT, University of Luxembourg, Luxembourg
Rene Rydhof Hansen	Aalborg University, Denmark
Sushil Jajodia	George Mason University, USA
Sjouke Mauw	University of Luxembourg, Luxembourg
Guy McCusker	University of Bath, UK
Per Håkon Meland	SINTEF ICT, Norway
Andreas L Opdahl	University of Bergen, Norway
Xinming Ou	University of South Florida, USA
Stephane Paul	Thales Research and Technology, France
Sophie Pinchinat	IRISA Rennes, France
David Pym	University College London, UK
Sasa Radomirovic	University of Dundee, UK
Marielle Stoelinga	University of Twente, The Netherlands
Jan Willemson	Cybernetica, Estonia

Additional Reviewers

Albanese, Massimiliano	Lê Cong, Sébastien
Allard, Tristan	Paul, Soumya
Horne, Ross	Schwarzentruber, François
Kumar, Rajesh	Widel, Wojciech

Intrusion Tolerance
in Complex Cyber Systems
(Invited Talk)

Mike Fisk

Chief Information Officer
Los Alamos National Laboratory, NM, USA
mike.fisk@lanl.gov

Abstract. In this talk, we will consider intrusion tolerance as a desirable property of cyber systems and discuss the relationship between intrusion tolerance and resilience. Intrusion-tolerant complex systems maintain certain security properties even when components of those systems are compromised. We will examine some ways to quantify intrusion tolerance using graphical models of complex cyber systems with a focus on the misuse of authentication credentials and the exploitation of trust relationships. Finally, we will provide some examples of the impact of this analysis on real-world policy decisions.

Contents

Tendrils of Crime: Visualizing the Diffusion of Stolen Bitcoins

Mansoor Ahmed[(✉)], Ilia Shumailov, and Ross Anderson

Department of Computer Science and Technology, University of Cambridge,
Cambridge, UK
{mansoor.ahmed,ilia.shumailov,ross.anderson}@cl.cam.ac.uk

Abstract. The first six months of 2018 have seen cryptocurrency thefts of $761 million, and the technology is also the latest and greatest tool for money laundering. This increase in crime has caused both researchers and law enforcement to look for ways to trace criminal proceeds. Although tracing algorithms have improved recently, they still yield an enormous amount of data of which very few datapoints are relevant or interesting to investigators, let alone ordinary bitcoin owners interested in provenance. In this work we describe efforts to visualize relevant data on a blockchain. To accomplish this we come up with a graphical model to represent the stolen coins and then implement this using a variety of visualization techniques.

Keywords: Bitcoin · Cybercrime · Cryptocrime · Visualization

1 Introduction

All Bitcoin transactions are written on the blockchain, a public append-only file. Tracing transactions might seem trivial, given the linear nature of the data structure. And there are already many visualizations of Bitcoin, ranging from simple diagrams of the transactions within each block to more involved projects showing clusters of communities within the network [1,4]. However, things are not so simple when one tries to analyse provenance information such as the flow of stolen coins.

We need to first understand the context of this research. The next section will provide some background on how Bitcoin transactions work. Next, we will look into what taint tracking is and why it is required; after that we will look at tracking techniques in the existing literature and why we chose one particular method. Next we introduce the difficulties with visualizing this tracking data and then present our solutions. We finally discuss the related work and conclude by pointing at avenues for future research.

2 Bitcoin Primer

In the interest of brevity, we abstract and simplify some of the relevant features of Bitcoin transactions. For a more thorough explanation, we direct the reader to the original paper [11] or to the standard textbook [12].

© Springer Nature Switzerland AG 2019
G. Cybenko et al. (Eds.): GraMSec 2018, LNCS 11086, pp. 1–12, 2019.
https://doi.org/10.1007/978-3-030-15465-3_1

2.1   Transactions

To perform a Bitcoin transaction, you must first locate an Unspent Transaction Output (UTXO) for which you have a signing key, and spend it by signing it over to someone else. Essentially, the total amount of bitcoin you can spend is the total amount of UTXOs attributed to public keys whose private keys are in your control.

More generally, each transaction in Bitcoin is a signed blob that is interpreted by Bitcoin's scripting system, called "Script". Each valid transaction consists of a set of input UTXOs, a set of signatures that verify using the public keys associated with those UTXOs, a set of output addresses, and an amount of cryptocurrency to be sent to each of the outputs.

It is impossible to subdivide a UTXO, so if Bob wants to pay Alice 0.5 bitcoins but his savings are in the form of a single UTXO worth 50 bitcoins, then he has to make a transaction with two outputs: one to Alice (for 0.5 bitcoins), and one to a change address owned by himself (for 49.5 bitcoins). As a result, many bitcoin transactions have multiple outputs, and public keys in bitcoin tend to be short-lived. It is standard practice for a wallet application to generate a new keypair for each transaction and use the public key as the change address.

Transactions can refer to UTXOs in blocks of many different ages. So while the first input to a transaction could be from the block immediately preceding the current one, the second could be from a block two years ago (roughly 50,000 blocks). Such hop lengths make temporal visualizations of bitcoin transactions quite problematic.

2.2   A Loose Transaction Taxonomy

For our purposes, we classify bitcoin transactions into the following types:

1-to-1 transactions
Transactions where a single UTXO is sent to a single output. These are often used as building blocks in more complex payment schemes.

Many-to-2 transactions
The workhorse of bitcoin transactions; as discussed, these are a natural consequence of the indivisibility of UTXOs, and most legitimate transactions belong in this category.

1-to-many transaction
These are quite rare since normal payments to multiple entities are executed by most wallets as a chain of transactions. 1-to-many transactions are often used in money-laundering schemes (also known as mixes) to split crime proceeds proceeds into many wallets in order to make tracing difficult.

Many-to-many transactions
These are like 1-to-many transactions except that they have multiple input UTXOs. They are the second component in a typical mix; they shuffle cryptocurrency between different keys, mostly controlled by the same people.

Where transactions have many inputs and the inputs are signed by different keys, this provides extra information to the analyst, namely that the keys in question were under the same control. Heuristics like this enable analysts to cluster related transactions [9].

3   Taint Tracking

A specialist analysis firm has reported that in the first six months of 2018, 761 million dollars' worth of cryptocurrencies have been stolen [14]. Even if we only count major reported thefts from exchanges, perhaps 6–9% of the bitcoins in circulation have been stolen at least once [7]; the true number is undoubtedly higher. If one is to make good the victims of these crimes, then we need to be able to track down stolen or otherwise tainted bitcoins.

Bitcoin tracing is also important for law enforcement officers, regulators and researchers investigating ransomware, sanctions busting, online drug trafficking and other crimes facilitated by cryptocurrency. And the legal status of a bitcoin UTXO may depend on its history. Referring to Figs. 1–3, the red taint might mean that a bitcoin was stolen, green that it passed through the hands of an Iranian company under international sanctions, blue that it passed through a mix in contravention of money-laundering regulations and yellow that it was used to buy and sell drugs on AlphaBay. In the first case, it will still normally belong to the theft victim, who could sue to recover it. In the second, third and fourth, its owner may be prosecuted under applicable law. In the second, an owner who was a banker might be at risk of losing their licence. In the fourth, it may also be liable to particularly stringent asset-forfeiture laws; any wallet containing drug proceeds may be seized in many jurisdictions, with the onus then falling on the owner to prove honest provenance of any sums they wish to recover.

3.1   Status Quo

For a while, Bitcoin researchers focused on two ways of doing tracing: poison and haircut. To illustrate the difference, suppose you have a wallet with three stolen bitcoin and seven freshly-mined ones. Then under poison all the coins you spend from this wallet are considered 100% stolen, while under haircut they are reckoned to be 30% stolen.

This goes across to multiple types of taint. In poison, if you have inputs with four different kinds of taint then all the outputs are tainted with everything. This leads to rapid taint contagion. Figure 1a illustrates poison tainting.

Haircut is only slightly different. Here, taint is not binary but fractional. So, instead of saying that all the outputs are tainted with the four kinds of taint, we associate a fractional value to the taint. If half of the input was tainted red then all the outputs are half red-tainted. Taint diffuses quickly through the network as in poison, but the result is rapid taint diffusion, rather than contagion. Figure 1b illustrates haircut tainting.

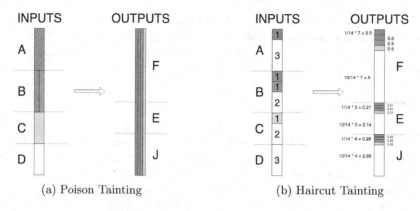

(a) Poison Tainting   (b) Haircut Tainting

Fig. 1. The long-standing methods proposed within the Bitcoin community for taint tracking. (Color figure online)

To put numbers to the diffusion, we ran poison and haircut on a couple of major thefts from 2014 and found that by 2017 more than 90% of wallets active on the network were tainted. This diffusion prevents any sensible recourse for victims – if we were to recover the 9% of stolen bitcoin and refund the victims, we might as well levy a 9% tax on all users. That is politically and technically impractical. What we need is a deterministic manner of tainting that does not diffuse wildly.

3.2 FIFO Taint Tracking

The diffusion problem is tackled by recent work by Anderson et al. [2,3]. They proceed from on Clayton's case – a legal precedent in London in 1816 and in force throughout the UK, Canada and many other Commonwealth countries. The judge in that case decided that funds whose ownership is under dispute must be tracked through accounts on a strict First-In-First-Out (FIFO) basis. A natural conclusion is that taint in a cryptocurrency should be tracked in this way. This greatly cuts the diffusion as taint is conserved. It is shown in Fig. 2.

Each bitcoin is divided into 100 million satoshi, and each satoshi is unique, in that it has a unique and public history. The data to enable tracing is built into the system; we just need the right algorithm to parse it; and FIFO appears to be that algorithm.

The FIFO principle is well-known in computer science as well as in law. FIFO tracking of disputed cryptocurrency turns out to be lossless and deterministically reversible. In addition to tracking a stolen bitcoin forwards – as one has to do with the poison or haircut methods – one can track a current UTXO backwards to all the reward blocks in which its component satoshi came into existence. This also makes for a much cleaner implementation. The tricky bit is the handling of transaction fees but once that's done, we can track the provenance of any satoshi.

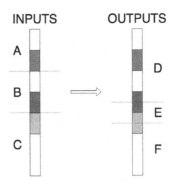

INPUTS   OUTPUTS

Fig. 2. FIFO tainting. (Color figure online)

3.3 Taintchain

We implemented FIFO tracking and built it into a system we call the taintchain. This starts off from a set of reported thefts or other crimes and propagates the taint backwards or forwards throughout the entire blockchain. If working forwards, start from all tainted transaction outputs and mark all the affected satoshis as tainted until you reach the end of the blockchain. If working backwards, trace each UTXO of interest backwards and if at any point you encounter a taint, then return taint for the affected satoshis. This was described in [2].

The visualization problem we tackle is how to analyse the data generated by the taintchain system[1].

4 Visualizing Taint

When we started analysing the taintchain, we ran into a number of issues. First is Big Data: just with 56 kinds of taint, we ended up with a dataset of about 450 GB. This grows about linearly as the user starts considering more crimes or more kinds of taints.

The second problem is that the things we're looking for – side effects of crime – are not always amenable to algorithmic analysis. Different criminals use different strategies to lauder their money; and mixes are designed to be difficult to deal with.

We surmised that a good visual representation of the data might help us to spot patterns. Moreover, it would possibly make the taintchain more usable – you could just enter your txhash and follow the taint.

4.1 Preliminary Model

Our first prototype used a simple graphical model for our taintchain data. We represented each transaction as a vertex and each hop as an edge. By hop, we

---

[1] Accessible at: https://github.com/TaintChain.

refer to the output of a transaction that has been used as an input somewhere else. Then we looked to represent our graph sensibly on-screen.

We decided to retain the chronological order and represent blocks as columns of transactions. Each transaction is a coloured rectangle where the colour reflects the kind of taint, and the size of rectangle reflects the number of satoshis tainted. Lastly, we decided to ignore clean satoshis as the data was sparse and required too much scrolling. We displayed this model as a static SVG graphic with click-to-reveal txhashes. Figure 3 shows an example.

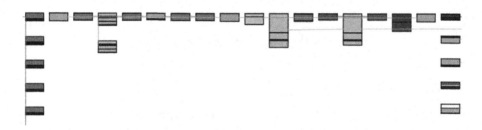

Fig. 3. An illustrative image from our preliminary visualization showing multitaint movement. (Color figure online)

To our surprise, even this rudimentary model gave us good results. We were able to spot quite a few interesting patterns via the visualization that we wouldn't have been able to see otherwise. For example, Fig. 4 shows someone collecting crime proceeds, that they had initially split to many addresses, into a single address. We call this a collection pattern and we observed similar patterns many times; in some of the instances, we were able to connect the collection address to illegal gambling sites.

Figure 5 shows the converse of a collection pattern: a splitting pattern. These may occur close to the time of a crime as criminals try to cover their tracks by feeding their loot into systems that divide their winnings into hundreds of tiny transactions.

4.2   Limitations of Preliminary Model

One of the main problems we faced was sheer data density. In Fig. 6 we are displaying only four kinds of taint and yet it is strenuous to follow the many lines. Increased spacing is not a solution here as that would result in an unmanageable amount of vertical scrolling.

Another problem we faced was that taint tends to overlap, as shown in Fig. 7. In that case, do we retain just one colour? Or do we create a new colour to represent the combination?

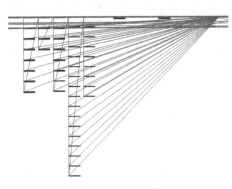

Fig. 4. A collection pattern

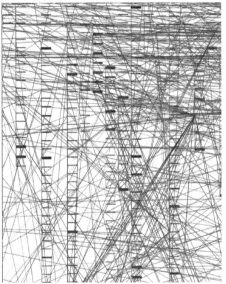

Fig. 5. A splitting pattern

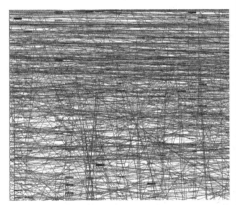

Fig. 6. Transaction density. The sheer number of tainted transactions renders some sections of the taintgraph uninterpretable.

Fig. 7. Complex collection pattern. We can see here the attempts by various actors to collect funds. However, this is difficult to spot due to the high degree of collocation of transactions. (Color figure online)

4.3   Interactive Visualization

We therefore decided to rethink our approach. The second prototype makes the graph interactive so the user can choose which information is relevant to her on the fly. Secondly, we decided to make the edges more meaningful. Rather than just show a connection between nodes, we incorporated the proportion of satoshis

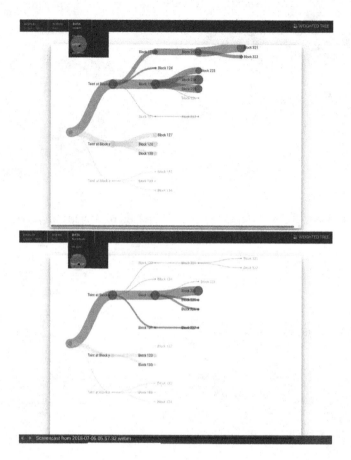

Fig. 8. These screenshots illustrate how the graph dynamically changes based on the taint type currently selected.

transferred in each hop into the edges. Lastly, we decided to abandon displaying the blocks as columns of transactions; instead we now focussed solely on the transaction flows and included the block information as a hint box displayed on mouse hover. Thus, now the depth of a vertex does not necessarily relate to its chronological order.

One of the problems that immediately vanished by the move to interactive representation was that of taint overlap. In our new system, we simply included a drop-down menu where the user can choose the taint type of interest and the graph adjusts its edges accordingly. Figure 8 shows this in action.

Making the graph interactive came at a cost, though, since now we want to store as much of the taintgraph in RAM instead of on disk for greater responsiveness. Second, since the graph expands on click, random exploration could lead to many uninteresting paths being followed.

We discovered some interesting patterns using this visualization. We were able to find multiple instances of *peeling chains*, as shown in Fig. 9. These are usually seen used by exchanges or gambling sites – in this case a notorious criminal exchange. Its operators would pool their money into a single wallet and then they would pay their customers successively, each time sending most of it to themselves at a change address. In this case, we can also see that this criminal exchange tried to hide their identity by shuffling their keys four times.

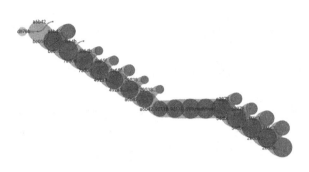

Fig. 9. A peeling chain, discovered by following the larger branch at each vertex.

However, although these visualisations are better than nothing, there still remains much to be done. A fundamental issue seems to be that of the large out-degree of some transactions. A transaction can have an (effectively) unbounded number of outputs, which makes visualizations difficult. Figure 10 illustrates this difficulty. One possible solution is to have a filter for transactions: collapse all the outputs below a certain threshold. This would give a cleaner display image, but might hamper investigations. We are still exploring effective aggregations that do not result in egregious information loss.

5   Related Work

A number of previous attempts have been made to visualize the Bitcoin network, with most of them focusing on some specific task. Early attempts were concerned with simple property representations e.g. Reid and Harrigan featured loglog plots of graph centrality measurements, graph representations with sizes of nodes showing the amounts of money transferred, geographical activity acquired through IP address mappings from Bitcoin Faucet, and graph representation of poison tainting [13].

Later came systems like BitIodine with graph-like outputs to support commonly available graph representation tools [15]. Graph approaches to transaction visualization were also adopted for educational purposes by systems like Coin-Vis [1], while bitcoin-tx-graph-visualizer used alluvial diagrams to show Bitcoin movement [8].

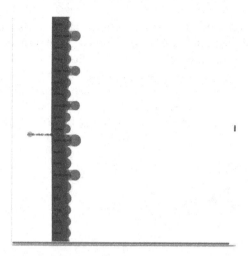

Fig. 10. Exhaustive vertical scrolling due to high outdegrees of transactions. Notice the scroll bar on the right.

A more mature system was BitConeView, presented by Battista and Donato in 2015 [4]. This was among the first to provide a sensible GUI to inspect how a particular UTXO propagated through the network. In order to explain what it means for money to move, the authors came up with 'purity' – basically a version of haircut tainting. They only evaluated the usability of their system informally, and came to the conclusion that more improvements were necessary to the way purity was presented to the user.

McGinn et al. devised a graph visualization of blockchain that allowed them to detect laundering activity and several denial-of-service attacks [5]. Unlike previous approaches, they made use of top-down system-wide visualization to understand transaction patterns. The follow-up paper from Molina et al. proposed an extension to a global view, in which graph analysis is aided by human intuition [10].

In our system we set out to learn from and build on all of this previous work. In particular, we focus on data representation in taint propagation when a taint graph becomes too massive for humans to comprehend.

Unlike BitConduit and similar systems, we are not doing any actor characterization in our visualisation tool [6]. The generation of graph colours is exogenous, relying on external theft reports or of software that analyses patterns of mixes, ransomware and other undesirable activity.

6 Future Work and Conclusion

In this short paper, we have presented a system for visualizing FIFO taint diffusion without any information-losing abstractions. This system has helped us spot interesting patterns that hint at the operational techniques of criminals operating on the Bitcoin network. We have made this system publicly available for anyone to use and modify.

It still suffers from a number of shortcomings that invite further work. One avenue for research would be to explore different heuristics to portray the data more concisely. One might aim at a system that presents a global, zoomed-out view of the data and successively introduces more information as the user explores a particular pattern on the blockchain. Another direction would be to highlight suspicious patterns of transactions automatically, for example, by marking coins that have recently emerged from a flurry of splits and merges. There are many other plausible heuristics to explore, a lot of data to analyse, and real social problems to tackle.

References

1. Aghaseyedjavadi, A., Bloomer, B., Giudici, S.: Coin viz
2. Anderson, R., Shumailov, I., Ahmed, M.: Making bitcoin legal. In: Twenty-Sixth International Security Protocols Workshop (2018)
3. Anderson, R., Shumailov, I., Ahmed, M., Rietmann, A.: Bitcoin redux. In: 17th Annual Workshop on the Economics of Information Security (2018)
4. Battista, G.D., Donato, V.D., Patrignani, M., Pizzonia, M., Roselli, V., Tamassia, R.: Bitconeview: visualization of flows in the Bitcoin transaction graph. In: 2015 IEEE Symposium on Visualization for Cyber Security (VizSec), pp. 1–8 (2015)
5. McGinn, D., Birch, D., Akroyd, D., Molina-Solana, M., Guo, Y., Knottenbelt, W.J.: Visualizing dynamic bitcoin transaction patterns. Big Data 4(2), 109–119 (2016)
6. Kinkeldey, C., Fekete, J.D., Isenberg, P.: BitConduite: visualizing and analyzing activity on the Bitcoin network. In: EuroVis 2017 - Eurographics Conference on Visualization, Posters Track (2017)
7. Lee, T.: A brief history of Bitcoin hacks and frauds. Ars Technica, 12 May 2017
8. Lu., W.: Bitcoin-tx-graph-visualizer. http://www.npmjs.com/package/bitcoin-tx-graphvisualizer
9. Meiklejohn, S., et al.: A fistful of Bitcoins: characterizing payments among men with no names. In: Proceedings of the 2013 Conference on Internet Measurement Conference, IMC 2013, pp. 127–140. ACM, New York (2013). https://doi.org/10.1145/2504730.2504747
10. Molina-Solana, M., Birch, D., Guo, Y.K.: Improving data exploration in graphs with fuzzy logic and large-scale visualisation. Appl. Soft Comput. 53, 227–235 (2017)
11. Nakamoto, S.: Bitcoin: a peer-to-peer electronic cash system (2008). http://bitcoin.org/bitcoin.pdf
12. Narayanan, A., Bonneau, J., Felten, E., Miller, A., Goldfeder, S.: Bitcoin and Cryptocurrency Technologies: A Comprehensive Introduction. Princeton University Press, Princeton (2016). https://books.google.co.uk/books?id=LchFDAAAQBAJ

13. Reid, F., Harrigan, M.: An analysis of anonymity in the Bitcoin system. In: 2011 IEEE Third International Conference on Privacy, Security, Risk and Trust and 2011 IEEE Third International Conference on Social Computing, pp. 1318–1326 (2011)

14. Reuters: Cryptocurrency exchange theft surges in first half of 2018: report. https:// reut.rs/2KLI3ow

15. Spagnuolo, M., Maggi, F., Zanero, S.: BitIodine: extracting intelligence from the Bitcoin network. In: Christin, N., Safavi-Naini, R. (eds.) FC 2014. LNCS, vol. 8437, pp. 457–468. Springer, Heidelberg (2014). https://doi.org/10.1007/978-3-662-45472-5_29

Deciding the Non-emptiness
of Attack Trees

Maxime Audinot[1], Sophie Pinchinat[1(✉)], François Schwarzentruber[1,2],
and Florence Wacheux[1]

[1] Univ. Rennes, IRISA, CNRS, Rennes, France
{maxime.audinot,sophie.pinchinat,florence.wacheux}@irisa.fr
[2] ENS Rennes, Rennes, France
francois.schwarzentruber@ens-rennes.fr

Abstract. We define and study the decision problem of the *non-emptiness* of an attack tree. This decision problem reflects the natural question of knowing whether some attack scenario described by the tree can be realized in (a given model of) the system to defend. We establish accurate complexity bounds, ranging from NP-completeness for arbitrary trees down to NLOGSPACE-completeness for trees with no occurrence of the AND operator. Additionally, if the input system to defend has a succinct description, the non-emptiness problem becomes PSPACE-complete.

1 Introduction

Attack trees are one of the most prominent graphical models for security, originally proposed by [20]. They are intuitive and provide a readable description of the (possibly many) ways of attacking a critical system, thus enabling efficient communication between security experts and decision makers.

For about a decade, formal methods have been deployed to tame these models, with the perspective to develop all kinds of assistant tools for attack trees. The formal approaches range among attack tree quantitative analysis [1,12], system-based approaches to assist experts in their design [2,3], and automated generation of attack trees [9,15,17]. All of these approaches rely on solid semantics. To cite a few, there are the multi-set semantics [14], the series-parallel graph semantics [11], the linear logic semantics [8], and the path/trace semantics [2,3].

It is important to notice that the path semantics of attack trees provides a natural way of interpreting the tree as a set of attacking scenarios in the system to defend. Such semantics therefore relies not only on the description of the tree but also on a formal definition of the system. This formal definition should reflect the evolution of the system when attacked, in other words its operational semantics. For example, in the ATSyRA tool [18] or in the Treemaker tool [10], the experts specify a system in some Domain Specific Language, then this specification is compiled into a transition system whose states denote the system configurations and whose transitions describe the ability for an attacker to act on the system, hence to modify the current configuration.

M. Audinot—This author was funded by DGA, Bruz.

G. Cybenko et al. (Eds.): GraMSec 2018, LNCS 11086, pp. 13–30, 2019.
https://doi.org/10.1007/978-3-030-15465-3_2

Although this is not made formal here, we claim that most of the existing semantics of attack trees in the literature intrinsically "contain" such an operational view of attack trees. It is therefore essential for further tools development to investigate computational aspects in terms of relevant decision problems such tools will need to solve.

One of the basic decision problems we can think of is addressed in the setting of the path semantics, and is called the *non-emptiness of an attack tree*, where the issue is to decide whether the tree describes a non-empty set of attacks on a given system or not. If the answer is no, then the expert is done because her attack tree describes ways of attacking that cannot be implemented by an attacker, meaning that the system is safe. Otherwise, the expert is informed that the system is vulnerable, and should carry on with her analysis. To our knowledge, there is currently no result regarding this question.

In this paper, we formalize this non-emptiness decision problem, establish tight computational complexity bounds, and discuss the impact of these results for tools development. More precisely, we show that:

1. For arbitrary attack trees, namely with no restrictions on the operators used in their description[1], this problem is NP-complete (Theorem 1);
2. Additionally to this general result, we consider the subclass of so-called *AND-free* attack trees, by disallowing the AND operator. For this subclass, we exhibit a polynomial-time algorithm to solve the non-emptiness problem (Theorem 4), and show that this restricted decision problem is NLOGSPACE-complete (Theorem 5);
3. Finally, we consider a variant of the non-emptiness decision problem where the input system has a symbolic presentation, as it is the case in most practical applications (see for example the tool ATSyRA [18]). We argue that the price to pay for this succinct way of specifying the system yields a PSPACE-complete complexity (Theorem 6).

The paper is organized as follows. We start by recalling the definition of transition systems in Sect. 2, and the central notions of concatenation and parallel decomposition of formal finite words needed to define the path semantics of attack trees in Sect. 3. Attack trees are introduced in Sect. 4, as well as the formal definition of the non-emptiness decision problem. Section 5 is dedicated to the non-emptiness problem for arbitrary attack trees, while Sect. 6 focuses on the subclass of AND-free attack trees. In Sect. 7, we discuss the case of symbolic transition systems, and conclude the contribution by pointing out some future work in Sect. 8.

2   Transition Systems

Let $Prop = \{\iota, \iota_1, \ldots, \gamma, \gamma_1 \ldots\}$ be a countable set of atomic propositions.

Definition 1. *A labeled transition system over Prop is a structure $\mathcal{S} = (S, \rightarrow, \lambda)$, where S is a finite set of states (whose typical elements are*

---
[1] Operators one can find in the dedicated literature, see Definition 5.

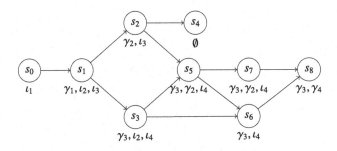

Fig. 1. A labeled transition system.

$s, s', s_0, s_1, \ldots$); $\rightarrow \subseteq S \times S$ *is the* transition relation, *and we write* $s \rightarrow s'$ *instead of* $(s, s') \in \rightarrow$; *and* $\lambda : Prop \rightarrow 2^S$ *is the* valuation *function that assigns a set of propositions to states.*

The size *of* $\mathcal{S}$ *is* $|\mathcal{S}| := |S| + |\rightarrow|$.

An example of labeled transition system with nine states $\{s_0, \ldots, s_8\}$ is depicted in Fig. 1. In such structures, paths are central objects as they represent the dynamic of the system.

Definition 2. *A* path *of* $\mathcal{S}$ *is a sequence* $\pi = s_0 \ldots s_n$ *of states of* $\mathcal{S}$, *such that* $n \geq 0$ *and* $s_i \rightarrow s_{i+1}$, *for every* $i < n$. *The set of paths of* $\mathcal{S}$ *is denoted* $\Pi(\mathcal{S})$.

In the following, we write $s \rightarrow^* s'$ whenever there exists a path $\pi = s_0 \ldots s_n$ with $s = s_0$ and $s' = s_n$.

We consider two notions on paths, namely *concatenation* and *parallel decomposition*, that will serve us to define the path semantics of attack trees. Because paths can be seen as finite words, i.e. finite sequence of states, we define these notions in the abstract setting of words.

3   Concatenation and Parallel Decomposition

We write $w(i)$ for the $(i+1)$-th letter of the word w, so that letter positions in words start at 0. Also, let $|w|$ be the *size* of w, so that $|w| - 1$ is its last letter position. We also write $w.first$ and $w.last$ for $w(0)$ and $w(|w| - 1)$ respectively, and for $[k, l] \subseteq [0, |w| - 1]$, we write $w[k, l] := w(k) \ldots w(l)$. A *factor* of a word w is a word w', such that $w[k, l] = w'$ for some $[k, l] \subseteq [0, |w| - 1]$, and we call interval $[k, l]$ an *anchoring* of w' in w; note w' may have several anchorings in w.

We now introduce the *concatenation of words* (Definition 3) and the *parallel decompositions of a word* (Definition 4). The concatenation w of two words w_1 and w_2 is similar to the usual notion of concatenation except that the last letter of w_1 and the first letter w_2 which should be the same are merged. Figure 2 shows the concatenation of words $s_0 s_2 s_7 s_1$ and $s_1 s_4 s_6$.

Definition 3 (Concatenation). *Let* w_1, w_2 *be two words of respective sizes* n_1 *and* n_2 *and such that* $w_1.last = w_2.first$. *The concatenation of* w_1 *and* w_2,

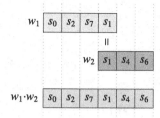

Fig. 2. Concatenation of words $s_0s_2s_7s_1$ and $s_1s_4s_6$.

denoted by $w_1 \cdot w_2$, is the word of size $n_1 + n_2 - 1$, where $w[0, n_1 - 1] = w_1$ and $w[n_1, n_1 + n_2 - 1] = w_2$. We naturally extend the definition of concatenation to sets of words: for two sets of words W_1 and W_2, we let $W_1 \cdot W_2 := \{w_1 \cdot w_2 \mid w_1 \in W_1 \text{ and } w_2 \in W_2\}$.

Intuitively, a parallel decomposition of a word w is the choice of a finite set of factors that entirely covers w. Figure 3a shows a possible parallel decomposition of the word $s_0s_2s_7s_1s_4s_6s_3$.

Definition 4 (Parallel decompositions of a word). *A set of words $\{w_1, \ldots, w_n\}$ is a* parallel decomposition *of a word w whenever the following holds.*

1. *For every $i \in [1, n]$, the word w_i is a factor of w at some anchoring $[k_i, l_i]$;*
2. *For every $j \in [0, |w| - 2]$, $[j, j+1] \subseteq [k_i, l_i]$, for some $i \in [1, n]$.*

The intervals $[k_i, l_i]$ form a covering *of $[0, |w| - 1]$.*

Notice that our notion of covering is stronger than the classic notion of interval covering which requires that the union of intervals $[k_i, l_i]$ matches $[0, |w| - 1]$. Indeed, Point 2 of Definition 4 requires that each 2-size factor of w is also a factor of some of the words w_i. In particular, the three words w_1, w_2, w_3 as chosen in Fig. 3b do not form a parallel decomposition of word $s_0s_2s_7s_1s_4s_6s_3$, since the 2-size word s_2s_7 is not a factor of any of these three words.

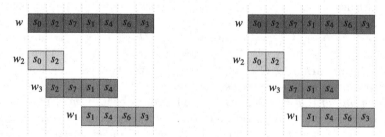

(a) Examples of words that form a parallel decomposition.

(b) Example of words that do not form a decomposition.

Fig. 3. Decomposition of word $s_0s_2s_7s_1s_4s_6s_3$.

We recall that $Prop = \{\iota, \iota_1, \ldots, \gamma, \gamma_1 \ldots\}$ is a countable set of atomic propositions, and we now define attack trees.

4   Attack Trees

In our formal setting, attack trees are finite labeled trees whose leaves are labeled by a pair $\langle \iota, \gamma \rangle$, where $\iota, \gamma \in Prop$ and whose internal nodes (non-leaves) are labeled by either symbol OR, symbol SAND (sequential and) or symbol AND. In our setting, and in most existing approaches in the literature, such labels correspond respectively to the union, the concatenation and the parallel decomposition of sets of paths (see Definition 6). W.l.o.g., we suppose that OR-nodes and SAND-nodes are binary, i.e. their nodes have exactly two children, since the corresponding semantics is associative (Definition 6). Figure 4 shows an attack tree with 4 leaves and 3 internal nodes.

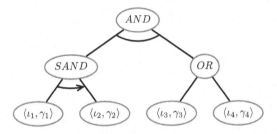

Fig. 4. Example of an attack tree.

Definition 5 (Attack tree). *An attack tree is defined by induction as follows.*

1. *A leaf labeled by a pair of propositions $\langle \iota, \gamma \rangle \in Prop \times Prop$ is an attack tree;*
2. *Given two attack trees τ_1 and τ_2, one can form the attack trees $OR(\tau_1, \tau_2)$ and $SAND(\tau_1, \tau_2)$;*
3. *Given a finite sequence $\tau_1, \tau_2 \ldots, \tau_n$ of attack trees, one can form the attack tree $AND(\tau_1, \ldots, \tau_n)$.*

An attack tree τ is *AND-free* if it is built only by means of Rules 1 and 2 of Definition 5. We will refer to a pair $\langle \iota, \gamma \rangle$ of propositions labeling the leaves of attack trees as a *reachability goal*, and to propositions ι and γ as the *precondition* and the *postcondition* of this reachability goal $\langle \iota, \gamma \rangle$ respectively.

An attack tree τ is interpreted in a transition system $\mathcal{S}$ as a set $[\![\tau]\!]^{\mathcal{S}}$ of paths in $\mathcal{S}$.

Definition 6 (Path semantics).   *The path semantics of τ in a transition system $\mathcal{S}$ is the set $[\![\tau]\!]^{\mathcal{S}} \subseteq \Pi(\mathcal{S})$ defined by induction as follows.*

- $[\![\langle \iota, \gamma \rangle]\!]^{\mathcal{S}} = \{\pi \in \Pi(\mathcal{S}) \mid \pi.first \in \lambda(\iota) \text{ and } \pi.last \in \lambda(\gamma)\}$

- $[\![OR(\tau_1, \tau_2)]\!]^{\mathcal{S}} = [\![\tau_1]\!]^{\mathcal{S}} \cup [\![\tau_2]\!]^{\mathcal{S}}$
- $[\![SAND(\tau_1, \tau_2)]\!]^{\mathcal{S}} = [\![\tau_1]\!]^{\mathcal{S}} \cdot [\![\tau_2]\!]^{\mathcal{S}}$
- $[\![AND(\tau_1, \tau_2, \ldots, \tau_n)]\!]^{\mathcal{S}}$ *is the set of paths π of $\mathcal{S}$ that admit a parallel decomposition $\{\pi_1, \pi_2, \ldots, \pi_n\}$ with $\pi_1 \in [\![\tau_1]\!]^{\mathcal{S}}, \ldots, \pi_n \in [\![\tau_n]\!]^{\mathcal{S}}$.*

Remark that the semantics for OR and SAND are associative because the corresponding operators on sets are. On the contrary, the semantics of AND is not associative, as shown in Example 1, and we therefore cannot restrict to a binary operator.

Example 1. Consider the system of Fig. 1. The set $[\![AND(\langle \iota_1, \gamma_1 \rangle, \langle \iota_4, \gamma_4 \rangle, \langle \iota_2, \gamma_2 \rangle)]\!]^{\mathcal{S}}$ contains the four paths $s_0 s_1 s_2 s_5 s_7 s_8$, $s_0 s_1 s_3 s_5 s_7 s_8$, $s_0 s_1 s_2 s_5 s_6 s_8$, and $s_0 s_1 s_3 s_5 s_6 s_8$, but $[\![AND(\langle \iota_1, \gamma_1 \rangle, \langle \iota_4, \gamma_4 \rangle)]\!]^{\mathcal{S}} = \emptyset$ because there is no state that is both on a path in $[\![\langle \iota_1, \gamma_1 \rangle]\!]^{\mathcal{S}}$ and on a path in $[\![\langle \iota_4, \gamma_4 \rangle]\!]^{\mathcal{S}}$, so that the set $[\![AND(AND(\langle \iota_1, \gamma_1 \rangle, \langle \iota_4, \gamma_4 \rangle), \langle \iota_2, \gamma_2 \rangle)]\!]^{\mathcal{S}}$ is also empty.

Now that attack trees are defined, we turn to the central problem of this contribution.

5   The Non-emptiness Problem for Attack Trees

The *non-emptiness decision problem for attack trees*, that we shortly call NON-EMPTINESS, is the following decision problem.

NON-EMPTINESS: Given a system $\mathcal{S}$ and an attack tree τ, do we have $[\![\tau]\!]^{\mathcal{S}} \neq \emptyset$?

Theorem 1. NON-EMPTINESS *is NP-complete.*

The rest of this section is dedicated to the proof of Theorem 1: we establish the NP upper bound in Subsect. 5.1 (Theorem 2), and in Subsect. 5.2, we resort to the result by [2] to obtain the NP lower bound (Theorem 3).

5.1   The Problem NON-EMPTINESS is NP-easy

We provide a non-deterministic polynomial-time algorithm (Algorithm 2) that answers the problem NON-EMPTINESS.

This algorithm, called nonemptiness$(\tau, \mathcal{S})$, relies on the *abstract semantics* (Definition 7) of attack trees, that consists only in sequences of *key states* that occur along paths of the path semantics. Notice that such sequences may not realize any path in $\mathcal{S}$, and will therefore be seen as words $w, w', \ldots \in S^*$.

Preliminarily to giving the definition of the abstract semantics of attack trees, we introduce the notion of *linearization* of a finite set of words: a linearization of words $w_1, \ldots, w_n$ is any word in the set $Lin(w_1, \ldots, w_n)$ defined as follows.

- If $n > 2$, then $Lin(w_1, \ldots, w_n) := Lin_2(Lin(w_1, \ldots, w_{n-1}), w_n)$;
- Otherwise $Lin(w_1, w_2) := Lin_2(w_1, w_2)$.

where $Lin_2(w_1, w_2)$ is defined inductively by: $Lin_2(\epsilon, \epsilon) := \epsilon$, and $Lin_2(sw, s'w')$ $:= s.Lin_2(w, s'w') \cup s'.Lin_2(s.w, w')$, to which we add $s.Lin_2(w, w')$ in case $s = s'$. For example, $Lin_2(s_2s_7, s_2s_4)$ contains $s_2s_7s_2s_4$, $s_2s_2s_4s_7$, and $s_2s_7s_4$.

Definition 7 (Abstract semantics). *The abstract semantics $[\![\tau]\!]^S_{abs} \subseteq S^*$ is defined by induction over τ:*

- $[\![\langle \iota, \gamma \rangle]\!]^S_{abs} = \{s_1s_2 \mid s_1 \models \iota, s_2 \models \gamma\}$;
- $[\![OR(\tau_1, \tau_2)]\!]^S_{abs} = [\![\tau_1]\!]^S_{abs} \cup [\![\tau_2]\!]^S_{abs}$;
- $[\![SAND(\tau_1, \tau_2)]\!]^S_{abs} = [\![\tau_1]\!]^S_{abs}.[\![\tau_2]\!]^S_{abs}$;
- $[\![AND(\tau_1, \ldots, \tau_n)]\!]^S_{abs}$ *contains all linearizations w of some words $w_1 \in [\![\tau_1]\!]^S_{abs}, \ldots w_n \in [\![\tau_n]\!]^S_{abs}$, such that every letter occurrence of w, but $w.first$ and $w.last$, either is strictly between $w_j.first$ and $w_j.last$ for some j, or equals both $w_j.first$ and $w_k.last$ for some $j \neq k$.*

Intuitively, $[\![\tau]\!]^S_{abs}$ contains *key states* in the sense that those are states satisfying the relevant pre/post-conditions appearing in the tree τ.

Example 2. Recall the labeled transition system of Fig. 1. The word s_2s_7 is in the set $[\![\langle \iota_3, \gamma_3 \rangle]\!]^S_{abs}$ since s_2 and s_7 are states satisfying the precondition ι_3 and the postcondition γ_3 respectively, but s_2s_7 is not a path in S. Because s_2s_7 is in $[\![\langle \iota_3, \gamma_3 \rangle]\!]^S_{abs}$ and s_7s_8 is in $[\![\langle \iota_4, \gamma_4 \rangle]\!]^S_{abs}$, the word $s_2s_7s_8$ belongs to $[\![SAND(\langle \iota_2, \gamma_2 \rangle, \langle \iota_4, \gamma_4 \rangle)]\!]^S_{abs}$.

Algorithm 2 `nonemptiness`(τ, S) consists in two steps:

(a) A call to the sub-routine `guessAbstractPath`(τ, S) (Algorithm 1) in order to guess a word w that plays the role of a *certificate* with key states;
(b) A check that w is "realizable" in S, i.e. that there exists a path between any two consecutive key states occurring in w.

Step (a) amounts to executing Algorithm 1, which non-deterministically guesses a word in $[\![\tau]\!]^S_{abs}$. In case of leaf tree $\langle \iota, \gamma \rangle$, the algorithm non-deterministically guesses two states s_1, s_2 and verifies the property that ι holds in s_1 and γ holds in s_2. If this property holds, Algorithm 1 returns the two-letter word s_1s_2, otherwise it rejects the input. For a tree of the form $OR(\tau_1, \tau_2)$, the algorithm non-deterministically guesses one of the two sub-trees, i.e., some $i \in \{1, 2\}$, and then recursively executes `guessAbstractPath`(τ_i, S). For a tree of the form $SAND(\tau_1, \tau_2)$, the algorithm guesses two words w_1 and w_2 in $[\![\tau_1]\!]^S_{abs}$ and $[\![\tau_2]\!]^S_{abs}$ respectively, and returns the word $w_1.w_2$ whenever $w_1.last = w_2.first$, otherwise it rejects the input. For the case of a tree of the form $AND(\tau_1, \ldots, \tau_n)$, the algorithm guesses words w_i in $[\![\tau_i]\!]^S_{abs}$, then it guesses a linearization of those, and finally verifies that this latter guess is indeed a linearization (see the **forall** loop in the last **case** of Algorithm 1).

The following proposition formally states the specification of Algorithm 1:

Proposition 1. – *Any non-rejecting execution of Algorithm 1 returns a word in $[\![\tau]\!]_{abs}^{\mathcal{S}}$.*
– *Reciprocally, for every word in $[\![\tau]\!]_{abs}^{\mathcal{S}}$, there exists a non-rejecting execution of Algorithm 1 that returns this word.*

Proof. The proof can be conducted by induction on τ and is left to the reader.

Input: An attack tree τ and a transition system $\mathcal{S}$
Output: A word $w \in [\![\tau]\!]_{abs}^{\mathcal{S}}$
switch τ do
  case $\langle \iota, \gamma \rangle$ do
    guess $s_1, s_2 \in S$;
    check $s_1 \in \lambda(\iota)$ and $s_2 \in \lambda(\gamma)$;
    return $s_1 s_2$;
  end
  case $OR(\tau_1, \tau_2)$ do
    guess $i \in \{1, 2\}$;
    return guessAbstractPath$(\tau_i, \mathcal{S})$;
  end
  case $SAND(\tau_1, \tau_2)$ do
    $w_1 :=$ guessAbstractPath$(\tau_1, \mathcal{S})$;
    $w_2 :=$ guessAbstractPath$(\tau_2, \mathcal{S})$;
    check $w_1.last = w_2.first$;
    return $w_1 \cdot w_2$
  end
  case $AND(\tau_1, \ldots, \tau_n)$ do
    $w_i :=$ guessAbstractPath$(\tau_i, \mathcal{S})$ for each $1 \leq i \leq n$;
    guess w, a linearization of $w_1, \ldots, w_n$;
    forall *letters s of w except $w.first$ and $w.last$* do
      check *there exist $j, k \in [1, n]$ such that either s is strictly between $w_j.first$ and $w_j.last$ in w, or s equals both $w_j.first$ and $w_k.last$*
    end
    return w;
  end
end

Algorithm 1. guessAbstractPath$(\tau, \mathcal{S})$.

Regarding Step (b) of Algorithm 2, the procedure consists in verifying that the word w resulting from Step (a) can be *realized by a path* in the system $\mathcal{S}$, in the sense that there exist sub-paths between every successive key states occurring in w (see Definition 8).

Definition 8. *Given a system $(S, \rightarrow, \lambda)$, a word $w = s_0 \ldots s_n \in S^*$ is* realized *by a path π in $\mathcal{S}$ if $\pi = \pi_0 \cdot \ldots \cdot \pi_{n-1}$ for some π_i's that are paths from s_i to s_{i+1} in $\mathcal{S}$ respectively. Notice that $w.first = \pi.first$ and $w.last = \pi.last$. Note also that any factor of w is also realizable.*

Verifying that the word is realizable by a path uses the Boolean function $\text{reach}_{\mathcal{S}}$ whose specification is: given two states $s_1, s_2 \in S$, $\text{reach}_{\mathcal{S}}(s_1, s_2)$ is true iff there is a path from s_1 to s_2 in $\mathcal{S}$. It is well known that such a function can be implemented in polynomial time.

Input: An attack tree τ and a transition system $\mathcal{S}$
Output: Accept whenever $[\![\tau]\!]^{\mathcal{S}} \neq \emptyset$.
//Step (a)
$w :=$ `guessAbstractPath`$(\tau, \mathcal{S})$;
//Step (b)
foreach s_1, s_2 *successive in* w **do**
  | check $\text{reach}_{\mathcal{S}}(s_1, s_2)$
end
accept

Algorithm 2. `nonemptiness`$(\tau, \mathcal{S})$.

The correctness of Algorithm 2 follows from Proposition 2:

Proposition 2. *The two following statements are equivalent:*

(i) There exists a word $w \in [\![\tau]\!]_{abs}^{\mathcal{S}}$ that can be realized by a path of $\mathcal{S}$;
(ii) $[\![\tau]\!]^{\mathcal{S}} \neq \emptyset$.

Proof. We show that (i) implies (ii) by establishing an inductive proof over τ that if $w \in [\![\tau]\!]_{abs}^{\mathcal{S}}$ can be realized by a path π of $\mathcal{S}$, then $\pi \in [\![\tau]\!]^{\mathcal{S}}$.

If $w \in [\![\langle \iota, \gamma \rangle]\!]_{abs}^{\mathcal{S}}$ then $w.first \models \iota$ and $w.last \models \gamma$, if w can be realized by some path π, then $w.first = \pi.first$ and $w.last = \pi.last$. One easily concludes that $\pi \in [\![\langle \iota, \gamma \rangle]\!]^{\mathcal{S}}$. If $w \in [\![\text{OR}(\tau_1, \tau_2)]\!]_{abs}^{\mathcal{S}}$, which by Definition 7, equals $[\![\tau_1]\!]_{abs}^{\mathcal{S}} \cup [\![\tau_2]\!]_{abs}^{\mathcal{S}}$, pick some i such that $w \in [\![\tau_i]\!]_{abs}^{\mathcal{S}}$. By induction hypothesis, we then get $\pi_i \in [\![\tau_i]\!]^{\mathcal{S}}$ that realizes w and because $[\![\tau_i]\!]^{\mathcal{S}} \subseteq [\![\text{OR}(\tau_1, \tau_2)]\!]^{\mathcal{S}}$, word w is realized by $\pi_i \in [\![\text{OR}(\tau_1, \tau_2)]\!]^{\mathcal{S}}$, which allows us to conclude. If $w \in [\![\text{SAND}(\tau_1, \tau_2)]\!]_{abs}^{\mathcal{S}}$, which by Definition 7, equals $[\![\tau_1]\!]_{abs}^{\mathcal{S}} \cdot [\![\tau_2]\!]_{abs}^{\mathcal{S}}$, then $w = w_1 \cdot w_2$, with $w_1 \in [\![\tau_1]\!]_{abs}^{\mathcal{S}}$ and $w_2 \in [\![\tau_2]\!]_{abs}^{\mathcal{S}}$. Since moreover w can be realized, so are its two factors w_1 and w_2, say by some paths π_1 and π_2. By induction hypothesis, $\pi_1 \in [\![\tau_1]\!]^{\mathcal{S}}$ and $\pi_2 \in [\![\tau_2]\!]^{\mathcal{S}}$. Now, $\pi_1.last = w_1.last = w_2.first = \pi_2.first$, word w is clearly realized by $\pi_1 \cdot \pi_2$ with $\pi \in [\![\text{SAND}(\tau_1, \tau_2)]\!]^{\mathcal{S}}$. The last case where $w \in [\![\text{AND}(\tau_1, \ldots, \tau_n)]\!]_{abs}^{\mathcal{S}}$ is tedious, and omitted here.

To show that (ii) implies (i), we establish by induction over τ that if $\pi \in [\![\tau]\!]^{\mathcal{S}}$, then there is a word $w \in [\![\tau]\!]_{abs}^{\mathcal{S}}$ that is realized by π.

Suppose $\pi \in [\![\langle \iota, \gamma \rangle]\!]^{\mathcal{S}}$, then clearly the word $(\pi.first)(\pi.last)$ is in $[\![\langle \iota, \gamma \rangle]\!]_{abs}^{\mathcal{S}}$, and is by construction realizable by π.

Suppose $\pi \in [\![\text{OR}(\tau_1, \tau_2)]\!]^{\mathcal{S}} = [\![\tau_1]\!]^{\mathcal{S}} \cup [\![\tau_2]\!]^{\mathcal{S}}$. Pick i such that $\pi \in [\![\tau_i]\!]^{\mathcal{S}}$. By induction hypothesis, there exists w that is realized by π and in $[\![\tau_i]\!]_{abs}^{\mathcal{S}} \subseteq [\![\text{OR}(\tau_1, \tau_2)]\!]_{abs}^{\mathcal{S}}$, which concludes the argument.

Suppose $\pi \in [\![\text{SAND}(\tau_1, \tau_2)]\!]^{\mathcal{S}}$. Pick $\pi_1 \in [\![\tau_1]\!]^{\mathcal{S}}$ and $\pi_2 \in [\![\tau_2]\!]^{\mathcal{S}}$ with $\pi = \pi_1 \cdot \pi_2$. By induction hypothesis, there is a word $w_1 \in [\![\tau_1]\!]_{abs}^{\mathcal{S}}$ that can be realized by

π_1, and similarly, there is a word $w_2 \in [\![\tau_2]\!]_{\text{abs}}^{\mathcal{S}}$ that can be realized by π_2. Since $w_1.last = \pi_1.last = \pi_2.first = w_2.first$, the word $w = w_1 \cdot w_2$ is well defined, clearly belongs to $[\![\text{SAND}(\tau_1, \tau_2)]\!]_{\text{abs}}^{\mathcal{S}}$, and is realized by π.

The case where $\pi \in \text{AND}(\tau_1, \ldots, \tau_n)$ is tedious and left to the reader.

Proposition 3. *Algorithm 2 is non-deterministic and runs in polynomial time.*

Proof. Clearly Step (a) makes at most one call to Algorithm 1 (which is non-deterministic and runs in polynomial time, see just below) per each node of the input tree, so Step (a) runs in time linear in the size of the input. Step (b) executes a call to the polynomial-time algorithm *Reach* at most a number of times bounded by the size of the word output in Step (a) – hence a polynomial number.

Regarding the complexity of Algorithm 1, the guesses made are either some $i \in \{1, 2\}$, or a pair of states, or some linearization of a set of words. All those have a polynomial size because the first is constant sized, the second in logarithmic in the size of the input system $\mathcal{S}$, and any linearization has a size at most twice the number of leaves in the input tree.

This concludes the proof of Proposition 3.

By Propositions 2 and 3, we obtain:

Theorem 2. NON-EMPTINESS $\in$ NP.

The next section completes the proof of Theorem 1.

5.2   The Problem NON-EMPTINESS is NP-hard

We inherit from the result [2, Proposition 2] that can be rephrased as follows in our context.

Theorem 3. NON-EMPTINESS *is NP-hard, even if we restrict to trees of the form AND($\langle \iota_1, \gamma_1 \rangle, \ldots, \langle \iota_n, \gamma_n \rangle$).*

The proof of Theorem 3 is based on a polynomial reduction from the propositional satisfiability problem to NON-EMPTINESS for trees of the form AND($\langle \iota_1, \gamma_1 \rangle, \ldots, \langle \iota_n, \gamma_n \rangle$). Because the former is NP-hard [7], so is the latter, NON-EMPTINESS.

We recall some basic vocabulary. Let $\{p_1, \ldots, p_r\}$ be a set of propositions. A *literal* ℓ is either a proposition p or its negation $\neg p$. A *clause* C is a disjunction of literals. The *propositional satisfiability problem* SAT is as follows.

Input: A set $\mathscr{C} = \{C_1, \ldots, C_m\}$ of clauses.
Output: Does there exist a valuation over *Prop* that satisfies the set of clauses $\mathscr{C}$?

Consider $\mathscr{C} = \{C_1, \ldots, C_m\}$, an instance of SAT, and let $\{p_1, \ldots, p_r\}$ be an ordering of the set of propositions occurring in the clauses of $\mathscr{C}$. It is standard to write $|\mathscr{C}|$ for the cumulative sum of the clauses' size, where the size of a clause is the number of its literals. In the following, we denote by ℓ_i an occurrence of proposition p_i or $\neg p_i$.

We define the labeled transition system $\mathcal{S}_\mathscr{C} := (S_\mathscr{C}, \to_\mathscr{C}, \lambda_\mathscr{C})$ over the set of propositions $Prop = \{start, C_1, \ldots, C_m\}$, where $start$ is a fresh proposition, as follows:

- The set of states is $S_\mathscr{C} = \bigcup_{i=1}^{r} \{p_i, \neg p_i\} \cup \{init\}$, where $init$ is a fresh state;
- The transition relation is $\to_\mathscr{C} = \{(init, \ell_1)\} \cup \{(\ell_i, \ell_{i+1}) \mid 1 \leq i \leq r - 1\}$;
- The labeling of states $\lambda_\mathscr{C} : \{start, C_1, \ldots, C_m\} \to 2^S$ is such that $\lambda_\mathscr{C}(start) = \{init\}$ and $\lambda_\mathscr{C}(C_i) = \{\ell \mid \ell \in C_i\}$ for every $1 \leq i \leq m$.

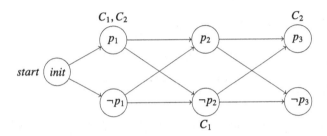

Fig. 5. The system $\mathcal{S}_{\{C_1, C_2\}}$ where $C_1 = p_1 \vee \neg p_2$ and $C_2 = p_1 \vee p_3$.

For example, the transition system corresponding to the set formed by the set of clauses $C_1 = p_1 \vee \neg p_2$ and $C_2 = p_1 \vee p_3$ is depicted in Fig. 5.

We now let the attack tree $\tau_\mathscr{C} := \text{AND}(\langle start, C_1 \rangle, \langle start, C_2 \rangle, \ldots, \langle start, C_m \rangle)$.

The reduction that we have described maps any instance $\mathscr{C} = \{C_1, \ldots, C_m\}$ of SAT to the instance $(\mathcal{S}_\mathscr{C}, \tau_\mathscr{C})$ of NON-EMPTINESS. It is trivially computable in polynomial time.

We now prove that $[\![\tau_\mathscr{C}]\!]^{\mathcal{S}_\mathscr{C}} \neq \emptyset$ if, and only if $\mathscr{C}$ is satisfiable.

($\Leftarrow$) Suppose that $\mathscr{C}$ is satisfiable. There exists a valuation over $Prop$ that satisfies a set of clauses $\mathscr{C}$. First, we consider the path that starts from $init$ and that follows the literals that are made true by this valuation. Second, we take the longest prefix π of that path that ends in a state labeled by C_j. As all C_i are satisfied by the valuation, all C_i appear on π, which shows $\pi \in [\![\tau_\mathscr{C}]\!]^{\mathcal{S}_\mathscr{C}}$.

($\Rightarrow$) Let $\pi \in [\![\tau_\mathscr{C}]\!]^{\mathcal{S}_\mathscr{C}}$. By definition of $\mathcal{S}_\mathscr{C}$, π cannot visit both a proposition and its negation. Therefore, π trivially denotes a partial valuation – that is completed by assigning false to all other propositions. Since $\pi \in [\![\tau_\mathscr{C}]\!]^{\mathcal{S}_\mathscr{C}}$, π visits a state labeled by C_i for every i, which shows that the valuation satisfies all the clauses. Hence, $\mathscr{C}$ is satisfiable.

6   The Non-emptiness Problem for AND-free Attack Trees

We here show that the complexity of deciding the non-emptiness of an attack tree boils down to NLOGSPACE if the input trees are AND-free. We write NON-EMPTINESS$_{Af}$ for this restricted version of the problem.

For a start, we establish that NON-EMPTINESS$_{Af}$ is in P (Theorem 4), and later in the section, we improve this bound by showing that NON-EMPTINESS$_{Af}$ is NLOGSPACE-complete (Theorem 5).

Theorem 4. NON-EMPTINESS$_{Af}$ *is in* P.

We prove Theorem 4 by developing the polynomial-time Algorithm 3 that answers NON-EMPTINESS$_{Af}$. This algorithm amounts to verifying the non-emptiness of the set returned by the the divide-and-conquer Algorithm 5, namely the set $\texttt{pairs}(\tau, \mathcal{S})$ of pairs of states in $\mathcal{S}$ that are ends (first and last states) of some path in $[\![\tau]\!]^{\mathcal{S}}$.

Input: An AND-free attack tree τ and a transition system $\mathcal{S} = (S, \rightarrow, \lambda)$
Output: $[\![\tau]\!]^{\mathcal{S}} \neq \emptyset$?
return $\texttt{pairs}(\tau, \mathcal{S}) \neq \emptyset$

Algorithm 3. $\texttt{nonemptinessAf}(\tau, \mathcal{S})$.

Before detailing Algorithm 5, we recall the simple Algorithm 4 used for the base case of leaf trees. This latter algorithm computes in polynomial time the set $\texttt{ends}(\iota, \gamma, \mathcal{S})$ of pairs of states that end a given path in $[\![\tau]\!]^{\mathcal{S}}$. Algorithm 4 calls $ReachableFrom_{\mathcal{S}}(s)$ which computes the set of states reachable from s in $\mathcal{S}$, that is the set of states s' such that $s \rightarrow^* s'$; clearly, the set $ReachableFrom_{\mathcal{S}}(s)$ can be computed in polynomial time in the size of $\mathcal{S}$.

Input: Two propositions $\iota, \gamma \in Prop$ and a transition system $\mathcal{S} = (S, \rightarrow, \lambda)$ over $Prop$
Output: The set $\{(s, s') \in S \times S \mid s \in \lambda(\iota), s' \in \lambda(s') \text{ and } s \rightarrow^* s'\}$
$P := \emptyset;$
foreach $s \in \lambda(\iota)$ **do**
$\quad | \quad P := P \cup \{s\} \times (ReachableFrom_{\mathcal{S}}(s) \cap \lambda(\gamma))$
end
return P

Algorithm 4. $\texttt{ends}(\iota, \gamma, \mathcal{S})$.

Since $\mathcal{S}$ is finite and since the size of the sets $\lambda(\iota)$ and $\lambda(\gamma)$ are less than or equal to the size of $\mathcal{S}$, and because $ReachableFrom_{\mathcal{S}}(s)$ is computable in polynomial time, we can claim the following.

Lemma 1. *Algorithm 4 terminates and its execution time is polynomial.*

It is also not hard to establish the correctness of Algorithm 4.

Lemma 2. *Algorithm 4 returns* $\{(s, s') \in S \times S \mid s \in \lambda(\iota), s' \in \lambda(s') \text{ and } s \to^* s'\}$.

We now describe the central Algorithm 5, which is defined by induction on τ.

Input: An AND-free attack tree τ and a transition system $\mathcal{S} = (S, \to, \lambda)$
Output: The set $\{(\pi.first, \pi.last) \mid \pi \in [\![\tau]\!]^{\mathcal{S}}\}$
switch τ do
    case $\langle \iota, \gamma \rangle$ do
      | return ends$(\iota, \gamma, \mathcal{S})$;
    end
    case $OR(\tau_1, \tau_2)$ do
      | return pairs$(\tau_1, \mathcal{S}) \cup$ pairs$(\tau_2, \mathcal{S})$
    end
    case $SAND(\tau_1, \tau_2)$ do
      return $\{ (s_1, s_2) \mid$ there exists s_3 such that $(s_1, s_3) \in$ pairs$(\tau_1, \mathcal{S})$ and
      $(s_3, s_2) \in$ pairs$(\tau_2, \mathcal{S})) \}$
    end
end

Algorithm 5. pairs$(\tau, \mathcal{S})$.

Lemma 3. *Algorithm 5 terminates and computes in polynomial time the set*

$$\{(s, s') \in S \times S \mid \text{ there exists } \pi \in [\![\tau]\!]^{\mathcal{S}} \text{ s.t. } s = \pi.first \text{ and } s' = \pi.last\}$$

Proof. The algorithm terminates since recursive calls are executed on smaller trees and the base case is a call to Algorithm 4 which terminates by Lemma 1. The correctness of Algorithm 5 can be established by conducting an inductive reasoning on τ while taking into account the semantics of the OR and SAND operators according to Definition 6. It is left to the reader. Regarding the time complexity of Algorithm 5, one can easily see that each node of the tree is visited once and that for each node the computation is in polynomial time, so that the overall time complexity remains polynomial.

We now can conclude the proof of Theorem 4 by observing that deciding the non-emptiness of an AND-free attack tree is equivalent to deciding pairs$_\mathcal{S}(\tau) \neq \emptyset$?, which can be achieved in polynomial time by Lemma 3 and the fact that verifying the non-emptiness of some set can be done in $O(1)$.

Actually, the optimal complexity of NON-EMPTINESS$_{Af}$ is the following.

Theorem 5. NON-EMPTINESS$_{Af}$ *is NLOGSPACE-complete.*

Input: An AND-free attack tree τ and a transition system $\mathcal{S}$
Output: Accept whenever $[\![\tau]\!]^{\mathcal{S}} \neq \emptyset$.
guess $s \in S$;
node := root of τ;
lastOp := *down*;
repeat
  if *node* = $\langle \iota, \gamma \rangle$ **then**
    check $s \models \iota$;
    loop
      guess whether we break the loop or not; if yes, **break** the loop;
      guess $s' \in S$ with $s \to s'$;
      $s := s'$
    endLoop
    check $s \models \gamma$;
  end
  if *(lastOp* = down*)* or *(lastOp* = over*)* **then**
    Try to perform and update *node* with operation *down, over, up* in priority order;
    Store in *lastOp* the last performed operation
  else
    Try to perform and update *node* with operation *over, up* in priority order;
    Store in *lastOp* the last performed operation
  end
until *(node* = root of τ*)* and *(lastOp* = up*)*;
accept

Algorithm 6. nonemptinessNL$_{ANDfree}(\tau, \mathcal{S})$.

Proof. The NLOGSPACE-hardness of NON-EMPTINESS$_{Af}$ follows from a trivial logspace reduction from the $s-t$-connectivity in an explicit graph – which is NLOGSPACE-complete according to [21] – to the non-emptiness of the path semantics of a leaf attack tree (of the form $\langle \iota, \gamma \rangle$).

For the NLOGSPACE-easiness, we describe Algorithm 6 which is a non-deterministic logspace algorithm that decides NON-EMPTINESS$_{Af}$. Algorithm 6 may look technical but its idea is simple: non-deterministically guess a path in $\mathcal{S}$ and simultaneously perform an exploration of the tree akin to a depth-first traversal. For SAND-nodes, perform the depth-first traversal as usual. For OR-nodes, guess one of the two children to explore while the other child is dismissed. When a leaf node $\langle \iota, \gamma \rangle$ is visited, non-deterministically extend the path with a suffix and check that the first state of this suffix is labeled by ι and that its last state is labeled by γ (see the first **if**-block in the **repeat**-loop).

The constructed path is not entirely stored: only its current last state s is memorized which requires a logarithmic number of bits in the size of $\mathcal{S}$. This exploration is implemented in logarithmic space via a technical trick similar to the one proposed in [13] for tree canonization.

Before explaining the variant of the depth-first traversal we use, we describe the technical trick for a standard depth-first traversal [13].

The traversal relies on three operations: *down*, *over*, *up*. The standard operations work as follows: operation *down* moves to the first child of the current node and fails if the current node has no children; operation *over* moves to the next sibling (left to right) of the current node and fails if the current node has no next sibling; operation *up* moves to the parent of the current node and fails if the current node is the root.

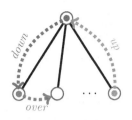

In order to visit only one child of an OR node, we modify the behavior of operations *down* and *over*; the behavior of operation *up* remains unchanged: if the current node is an OR-node, operation *down* guesses a child and moves to it; if the parent of the current node is an OR node, operation *over* always fails (instead of moving to the next sibling). The obtained modification of the depth-first traversal is such that exactly one child of an OR node is non-deterministically chosen and visited.

Algorithm 6 starts its exploration at the root of the attack tree and guesses a starting state s in $\mathcal{S}$. During the execution of the algorithm, variable s stores the last state in the current guessed path, variable *node* stores the current visited node in the tree and *lastOp* stores the last operation that was performed. At the beginning, we consistently suppose (by convention) that operation *down* has been performed. The **repeat**-loop performs the modified traversal of the attack tree. As already mentioned above, the first **if**-block treats a leaf $\langle \iota, \gamma \rangle$: it non-deterministically moves forward in the path and checks that the built path complies with the pre/post-conditions ι and γ. The second **if**-block controls the depth-first traversal. The **repeat**-loop ends when the traversal is finished, namely when the current node is the root of τ and the last operation is *up*.

7 The Case of Symbolic Transition Systems

So far in this paper, we have assumed that the system $\mathcal{S}$ is described in extension. However, in realistic applications, this explicit description may be huge owing to the classic state explosion problem. A way to circumvent this explosion is to represent systems in an implicit manner, known as *symbolic transition systems*. Typical symbolic representations are data structures such as BDDs [5] or languages such as STRIPS [6].

We introduce the decision problem NON-EMPTINESS$_{symb}$ akin to NON-EMPTINESS but where the input system is given symbolically. The price to pay for dealing with a succinct presentation of the system $\mathcal{S}$ yields the following increase of complexity.

Theorem 6. NON-EMPTINESS$_{symb}$ *is PSPACE-complete.*

Regarding the PSPACE-hardness of NON-EMPTINESS$_{symb}$, it is known that the *symbolic reachability problem*, i.e. knowing if in a symbolic transition system there exists some path from a given set of source states to a set of target states, is PSPACE-complete [6]. As an immediate consequence, deciding the non-emptiness of attack trees is already PSPACE-hard for leaf trees, i.e. whether $[\![\langle \iota, \gamma \rangle]\!]^{\mathcal{S}} \neq \emptyset$.

Concerning the PSPACE-easiness of NON-EMPTINESS$_{symb}$, we can adapt Algorithms 1 and 2 for NON-EMPTINESS as follows. First, guessing a state s of $\mathcal{S}$ is performed by guessing the polynomial number of bits that encode s in the symbolic representation of $\mathcal{S}$; this information is logarithmic in the exponential number of states denoted by the symbolic transition system, hence this information has a size that is polynomial in the size of the symbolic system. Second, checking $\mathrm{reach}_{\mathcal{S}}(s_1, s_2)$ is an instance of the symbolic reachability problem, known to be computable by an algorithm running in polynomial space [6].

All in all, those adaptations of Algorithms 1 and 2 yield an algorithm that is non-deterministic with a logspace complexity. This shows that the problem NON-EMPTINESS$_{symb}$ is in NPSPACE. Invoking Savitch's Theorem [19] that states the equality of the two complexity classes NPSPACE and PSPACE is enough to conclude.

8 Conclusion and Future Work

We have addressed the very natural decision problem of the non-emptiness of an attack tree, which involves an input tree and an input transition system, and we have studied its computational complexity. Mainly, the problem is (1) NP-complete for arbitrary trees, (2) NLOGSPACE-complete if we restrict to AND-free trees, and (3) PSPACE-complete for arbitrary trees and symbolic transition systems.

Regarding the most general problem NON-EMPTINESS with no restriction on attack trees, the established NP upper bound (Theorem 4) means that when the system is represented explicitly and is of "reasonable" size, it is relevant to consider implementations based on one (or a combination) of the following intelligent search algorithmic techniques: backtracking, backjumping, integer linear programming, reduction to SAT, use of SMT solvers. The use of a SAT solver could be used to encode the AND-constraints (parallel decomposition). Actually, it has already been successfully applied for a related problem in [3]: deciding the membership of a path in the semantics of an attack tree τ with respect to a system $\mathcal{S}$, formally "$\pi \in [\![\tau]\!]^{\mathcal{S}}$?".

Regarding our complexity results for the problem NON-EMPTINESS$_{Af}$, for the case of AND-free attack trees, we first showed that it is in P (Theorem 4), which means that we have an efficient algorithm. Even better, we showed that it is in NLOGSPACE (Theorem 5). Because the class NLOGSPACE falls within NC (Nick's class) [16, Theorem 16.1], the problem NON-EMPTINESS$_{Af}$ can be efficiently solved on parallel architectures (see [16, p. 376]).

In the future, we plan to resort to solvers to design and implement a reasoning tool on the non-emptiness of attack trees. Actually, such a reasoning tool also requires to solve the reachability problem (see the procedure $\mathrm{reach}_{\mathcal{S}}$ used in Algorithm 2). For these reasons, we will not only use a mere SAT solver but intend to draw on the $DPLL(T)^2$ architecture [4] of Satisfiability Modulo Theory (SMT) solvers. In our case, the theory T would be the system S itself, over which we solve the reachability problem. While an SMT solver architecture decomposes into a SAT solver and a decision procedure for T, our case would rather require an architecture decomposed into a SAT solver and a model checker. On the one hand, the constraints reflected by the abstract semantics $[\![\tau]\!]_{abs}^{S}$ may be solved by the SAT solver that returns a possible valuation reflecting a word $w \in [\![\tau]\!]_{abs}^{S}$. On the other hand, the model checker would verify that word w can be realized by a path in the system S. Similarly to what is done in SMT solvers, the SAT solver and the model checker will exchange information: the SAT solver provides elements $w \in [\![\tau]\!]_{abs}^{S}$ to the model checker and the model checker informs the SAT solver when a w is inconsistent within S. Interestingly, such an approach would synthesize a "witness" path of any non-empty attack tree.

References

1. Aslanyan, Z., Nielson, F.: Model checking exact cost for attack scenarios. In: Maffei, M., Ryan, M. (eds.) POST 2017. LNCS, vol. 10204, pp. 210–231. Springer, Heidelberg (2017). https://doi.org/10.1007/978-3-662-54455-6_10
2. Audinot, M., Pinchinat, S., Kordy, B.: Is my attack tree correct? In: Foley, S.N., Gollmann, D., Snekkenes, E. (eds.) ESORICS 2017. LNCS, vol. 10492, pp. 83–102. Springer, Cham (2017). https://doi.org/10.1007/978-3-319-66402-6_7
3. Audinot, M., Pinchinat, S., Kordy, B.: Guided design of attack trees: a system-based approach - to be published. In: 31th IEEE Computer Security Foundations Symposium, CSF 2018. IEEE (2018)
4. Barrett, C.W., Sebastiani, R., Seshia, S.A., Tinelli, C.: Satisfiability modulo theories. In: Handbook of Satisfiability, pp. 825–885. IOS Press, Amsterdam (2009)
5. Bryant, R.E.: Graph-based algorithms for Boolean function manipulation. IEEE Trans. Comput. **35**(8), 677–691 (1986)
6. Bylander, T.: The computational complexity of propositional STRIPS planning. Artif. Intell. **69**(1–2), 165–204 (1994)
7. Cook, S.A.: The complexity of theorem-proving procedures. In: Proceedings of the Third Annual ACM Symposium on Theory of Computing, pp. 151–158. ACM (1971)
8. Horne, R., Mauw, S., Tiu, A.: Semantics for specialising attack trees based on linear logic. Fundam. Inform. **153**(1–2), 57–86 (2017)
9. Ivanova, M.G., Probst, C.W., Hansen, R.R., Kammüller, F.: Attack tree generation by policy invalidation. In: Akram, R.N., Jajodia, S. (eds.) WISTP 2015. LNCS, vol. 9311, pp. 249–259. Springer, Cham (2015). https://doi.org/10.1007/978-3-319-24018-3_16
10. Ivanova, M.G., Probst, C.W., Hansen, R.R., Kammüller, F.: Transforming graphical system models to graphical attack models. In: Mauw, S., Kordy, B., Jajodia, S. (eds.) GraMSec 2015. LNCS, vol. 9390, pp. 82–96. Springer, Cham (2016). https://doi.org/10.1007/978-3-319-29968-6_6

---

[2] Where DPLL stands for Davis-Putnam-Logemann-Loveland and T is a first-order theory.

11. Jhawar, R., Kordy, B., Mauw, S., Radomirović, S., Trujillo-Rasua, R.: Attack trees with sequential conjunction. In: Federrath, H., Gollmann, D. (eds.) SEC 2015. IAICT, vol. 455, pp. 339–353. Springer, Cham (2015). https://doi.org/10.1007/978-3-319-18467-8_23

12. Kumar, R., Ruijters, E., Stoelinga, M.: Quantitative attack tree analysis via priced timed automata. In: Sankaranarayanan, S., Vicario, E. (eds.) FORMATS 2015. LNCS, vol. 9268, pp. 156–171. Springer, Cham (2015). https://doi.org/10.1007/978-3-319-22975-1_11

13. Lindell, S.: A logspace algorithm for tree canonization (extended abstract). In: Proceedings of the 24th Annual ACM Symposium on Theory of Computing, Victoria, British Columbia, Canada, 4–6 May 1992, pp. 400–404 (1992)

14. Mauw, S., Oostdijk, M.: Foundations of attack trees. In: Won, D.H., Kim, S. (eds.) ICISC 2005. LNCS, vol. 3935, pp. 186–198. Springer, Heidelberg (2006). https://doi.org/10.1007/11734727_17

15. Nielson, H.R., Nielson, F., Vigo, R.: Discovering, quantifying, and displaying attacks. Log. Meth. Comput. Sci. 12 (2016)

16. Papadimitriou, C.H.: Computational Complexity. Academic Internet Publ., Ventura (2007)

17. Pinchinat, S., Acher, M., Vojtisek, D.: Towards synthesis of attack trees for supporting computer-aided risk analysis. In: Canal, C., Idani, A. (eds.) SEFM 2014. LNCS, vol. 8938, pp. 363–375. Springer, Cham (2015). https://doi.org/10.1007/978-3-319-15201-1_24

18. Pinchinat, S., Acher, M., Vojtisek, D.: ATSyRa: an integrated environment for synthesizing attack trees. In: Mauw, S., Kordy, B., Jajodia, S. (eds.) GraMSec 2015. LNCS, vol. 9390, pp. 97–101. Springer, Cham (2016). https://doi.org/10.1007/978-3-319-29968-6_7

19. Savitch, W.J.: Relationships between nondeterministic and deterministic tape complexities. J. Comput. Syst. Sci. 4(2), 177–192 (1970)

20. Schneier, B.: Attack trees: modeling security threats. Dr. Dobb's J. Softw. Tools 24(12), 21–29 (1999)

21. Sipser, M.: Introduction to the Theory of Computation. PWS Publishing Company, Boston (1997)

Combining Bayesian Networks and Fishbone Diagrams to Distinguish Between Intentional Attacks and Accidental Technical Failures

Sabarathinam Chockalingam[1]([✉]), Wolter Pieters[1], André Teixeira[2], Nima Khakzad[1], and Pieter van Gelder[1]

[1] Faculty of Technology, Policy and Management, Delft University of Technology, Delft, The Netherlands
{S.Chockalingam,W.Pieters,N.KhakzadRostami,P.H.A.J.M.vanGelder}@tudelft.nl
[2] Department of Engineering Sciences, Uppsala University, Uppsala, Sweden
Andre.Teixeira@angstrom.uu.se

Abstract. Because of modern societies' dependence on industrial control systems, adequate response to system failures is essential. In order to take appropriate measures, it is crucial for operators to be able to distinguish between intentional attacks and accidental technical failures. However, adequate decision support for this matter is lacking. In this paper, we use Bayesian Networks (BNs) to distinguish between intentional attacks and accidental technical failures, based on contributory factors and observations (or test results). To facilitate knowledge elicitation, we use extended fishbone diagrams for discussions with experts, and then translate those into the BN formalism. We demonstrate the methodology using an example in a case study from the water management domain.

Keywords: Bayesian Network · Fishbone diagram ·
Intentional attack · Safety · Security · Technical failure

1 Introduction

Today's society depends on the seamless operation of Critical Infrastructures (CIs) in different sectors such as energy, transportation, and water management, which is essential to the success of modern economies. Over the years, CIs have heavily relied on Industrial Control Systems (ICS) to ensure efficient operations, which are responsible for monitoring and steering industrial processes as, among others, water treatment and distribution, and flood control.

Modern ICS no longer operates in isolation, but uses other networks to facilitate and improve business processes [23]. For instance, ICS uses internet to facilitate remote access to vendors and support personnel. This increased connectivity, however, makes ICS more vulnerable to cyber-attacks. The German

© Springer Nature Switzerland AG 2019
G. Cybenko et al. (Eds.): GraMSec 2018, LNCS 11086, pp. 31–50, 2019.
https://doi.org/10.1007/978-3-030-15465-3_3

steel mill incident is a typical example of a cyber-attack in which adversaries made use of corporate network to enter into the ICS network [35]. As an initial step, the adversaries used both the targeted email and social engineering techniques to acquire credentials for the corporate network. Once they acquired credentials for the corporate network, they worked their way into the plant's control system network and caused damage to the blast furnace.

It is essential to distinguish between (intentional) attacks and (accidental) technical failures that would lead to abnormal behavior in a component of the ICS and take suitable measures. However, there are challenges to achieve these goals. One particularly important challenge is that the abnormal behavior in a component of the ICS due to attacks is often initially diagnosed as a technical failure [28]. This could be due to the imbalance in the frequency of attacks and technical failures. On the other hand, this could be based on one of the myths of ICS security: *"our facility is not a target"* [21]. In most cases, the initiation of response strategy aimed at technical failures would be ineffective in case of a targeted attack, and may lead to further complications. For instance, replacing a sensor that is sending incorrect measurement data with a new sensor would be a suitable response strategy to technical failure of a sensor. However, this may not be an appropriate response strategy to an attack on the sensor as it would not block the corresponding attack vector. Furthermore, the initiation of inappropriate response strategies would delay the recovery of the system from adversaries and might lead to harmful consequences. Noticeably, there is a lack of decision support to distinguish between attacks and technical failures.

Bayesian Networks (BNs) can be potentially used to tackle the challenge of distinguishing attacks and technical failures as they enable diagnostic reasoning, which could help to identify the most likely cause of an event based on certain symptoms (or effects) [24]. The diagnostic inference capability of BN has been widely employed in real-world applications especially in medical diagnosis [31], and fault diagnosis [30]. However, BNs are difficult to interpret for ICS domain experts and are therefore unsuitable for extracting the necessary knowledge. Conversely, fishbone diagrams are easy-to-use for brainstorming with experts [9], but lack essential capacities for diagnostic inference. Therefore, fishbone diagrams can be potentially combined with BNs to suit the purposes of present challenge. This research aims to provide decision support for distinguishing between attacks and technical failures by addressing the research question: "How could we combine Bayesian Networks and Fishbone Diagrams to find out whether an abnormal behavior in a component of the ICS is due to (intentional) attack or (accidental) technical failure or neither?". The research objectives are:

- **RO1.** To develop a framework for constructing BN models for determining the major cause of an abnormal behavior in a component of the ICS.
- **RO2.** To leverage fishbone diagrams for knowledge elicitation within our BN framework, and demonstrate the application of the developed methodology via a case study.

The scope of our BN framework development is the choice of appropriate types of variables and relationships between the determined variables. Firstly, we identify appropriate types of variables from existing diagnostic BN models in other domains and adapt them to the purposes of the present study (i.e., distinguishing attacks and technical failures); accordingly, the relationships between the selected variables should be established. Furthermore, we provide a systematic method for incorporating fishbone diagrams within our BN framework to effectively elicit knowledge from different sources.

The remainder of this paper is structured as follows: Sect. 2 provides an essential foundation of diagnostic BNs and previous related work, followed by an overview of the state-of-the-art regarding fishbone diagrams in Sect. 3. In Sect. 4, we illustrate the different layers and components of ICS and describe the case study in the water management domain that is used to demonstrate our proposed methodology. In Sect. 5, our BN framework is developed with appropriate types of variables and the relationships between these variables are established. Furthermore, we demonstrate the application of the developed methodology to a case study in the water management domain in Sect. 5. Section 6 presents the conclusions and future work directions.

2   Diagnostic Bayesian Networks

This section explains diagnostic BNs with an example, and reviews existing diagnostic BNs in different domains. BNs belong to the family of probabilistic graphical models [2]. BNs consist of a qualitative and a quantitative part [7]. The qualitative part is a directed acyclic graph consisting of nodes and edges. Each node represents a random variable, while the edges between the nodes represent the conditional dependencies among the random variables. The quantitative part takes the form of a priori marginal and conditional probabilities so as to quantify the dependencies between connected nodes. An example of a BN model, representing the causal relationships between the risk factor "Smoking", the diseases "Bronchitis" and "Lung Cancer", and the symptoms "Shortness of Breath" and "Fatigue", is shown in Fig. 1(a).

When more evidence or information becomes available for some variables in the BN, the probabilities of other variables in the BN could be updated. This is called probability propagation, inference, or belief updating [24]. In the example shown in Fig. 1(b), the physician provides the evidence (via observation or supposition) for the symptoms "Shortness of Breath = False" and "Fatigue = True". Based on such evidence, the BN computes the posterior (updated) probabilities of the other nodes using Bayes' theorem. The BN in Fig. 1(b) determines that the absence of shortness of breath and the presence of fatigue are more likely due to lung cancer than bronchitis. In this case, we had evidence for symptoms (or effects) and inferred the most likely cause. This is called diagnostic or bottom-up reasoning. BNs also support three other types of reasoning: (i) Predictive or top-down: reasoning from causes to symptoms, (ii) Intercausal: reasoning about mutual causes of a common effect, and (iii) Combined: combination of different types of the above-mentioned reasoning [24].

BN models have widely been used for diagnostic analysis in different domains including agriculture [3], cyber security [25,26,33,38], health care [6,11,13,20,

29, 32, 39], and transportation [16, 19, 22]. Chen et al. [3] proposed a two-layer BN for maize disease diagnosis. In their model, the upper layer consists of diseases and the lower layer consists of symptoms. However, their BN model did not take into account other variables like risk factors. In this case, it could be difficult to diagnose a particular disease among other potential diseases with the same symptoms.

Pecchia et al. [33] developed a two-layer naïve BN model for detecting compromised users in shared computing infrastructures. In their model, the upper layer consists of a hypothesis variable "the user is compromised" while the lower layer consists of information variables. When more evidence or information becomes available for the information variables, this BN would help to diagnose whether the user has been compromised. In contrast to the BN model developed by Chen et al. [3], the upper layer consists of only one variable.

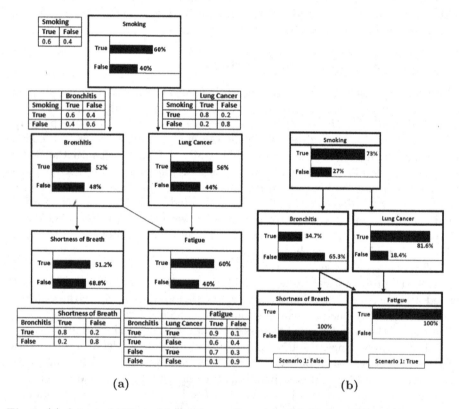

Fig. 1. (a) A typical BN model for disease diagnosis. (b) Updated probabilities given observed symptoms (evidence).

Oniśko et al. [32] proposed a three-layer BN for multiple-disorder diagnosis. In their model, the upper layer consists of risk factors, the middle layer consists of disorders, and the lower layer consists of symptoms and test results. In contrast to the BN models developed by Chen et al. [3] and Pecchia et al. [33], their BN model takes into account risk factors. Curiac et al. [6] also proposed a similar three-layer BN model for psychiatric disease diagnosis.

Huang et al. [16] proposed a four-layer BN for fault diagnosis of vehicle info-tainment system. In their work, the upper layer consists of root causes, the middle layer consists of intermediate nodes which are usually the group or cate-gory of the root causes, and two lower layers being distinguished with different colours. One of the lower layers consists of observations (or test results) while the other consists of a symptom. In contrast to the BN models proposed by Oniśko et al. [32] and Curiac et al. [6], their BN model did not take into account risk factors. On the other hand, their BN model considered observations (or test results) and symptom as separate layers. The observations (or test results) nodes could better help the diagnostic technicians who were not familiar with the list of diagnostic tests to be performed for diagnosing a particular root cause in the BN. The accuracy of posterior probabilities of non-evidenced variables in the BN would be improved as the observations (or test results) would make more evidence or information available based on the results of diagnostic tests performed.

Huang et al. [16] defined symptom as the failure symptom reported by the customer such as "no-sound", "no-display" in their vehicle infotainment system. In addition, they defined observations as any information useful for allocating the root causes such as those mentioned in the customer's reports or the outcomes of tests performed by diagnostic technicians. However, there is no clear distinction between the information from customer's reports that could be used to determine the observation nodes and a symptom node in the BN construction.

3   Fishbone Diagrams

This section explains fishbone diagrams, and highlights their application in both safety and security. Fishbone diagrams help to systematically identify and organ-ise the possible contributing factors (or sub-causes) of a particular problem [8,9,17,18,40]. Figure 2 shows the generic structure of a fishbone diagram, con-sisting of a problem and its possible contributing factors (or sub-causes) sorted and related under different categories. Each category represents the major cause of the problem. The categories used in the fishbone diagram depend on the classification scheme used for that application. In general, the arrows in the fish-bone diagram represent the causal relation between the causes and the problem (effect). The major advantages of fishbone diagram include: (i) fishbone diagrams are easily adaptable based on the discussions during brainstorming sessions [9], (ii) fishbone diagram encourages and guides data collection by showing where knowledge is lacking [9,17], (iii) fishbone diagram structure stimulates group participation [9,17], (iv) fishbone diagram structure helps to stay focused on the content of the problem during brainstorming sessions [9].

Fishbone diagrams are used in security and safety applications [1,27,41,42]. Asllani et al. [1] used fishbone diagrams to identify possible contributory fac-tors of network failure/intrusions, and used six different categories to sort

and relate contributory factors. For instance, they considered the problem as
"Network Failure/Intrusions" and one of the potential contributory factors as
"Antivirus Update" under the category "Processes". This implies that not
updating antivirus could contribute to network failure/intrusions. Zhao et al.
[41] used fishbone diagrams to illustrate possible contributory factors of tower
crane accidents under five different categories. Luca et al. [27] used fishbone
diagrams to illustrate possible contributory factors of noisy functioning of an
automotive flue gas system under four different categories. Zhu et al. [42] used
fishbone diagrams to illustrate possible contributory factors of crude oil vapors
explosion in the drain under six different categories.

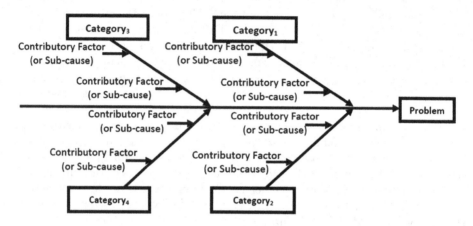

Fig. 2. Generic fishbone diagram structure

4   Industrial Control Systems

In this section, we illustrate the three different layers and major components in
each layer of ICS. Furthermore, we provide an overview of a case study in the
water management domain.

4.1   ICS Architecture

Domain knowledge on ICS is the starting point for the development and application of our BN framework. A typical ICS consists of three layers: (i) Field
instrumentation layer, (ii) Process control layer, and (iii) Supervisory control
layer [10], bound together by network infrastructure, as shown in Fig. 3.

The field instrumentation layer consists of sensors (S_i) and actuators (A_i),
while the process control layer consists of Programmable Logic Controllers
(PLCs)/Remote Terminal Units (RTUs). Typically, PLCs have wired communication capabilities whereas RTUs have wired or wireless communication capabilities. The PLC/RTU receives measurement data from sensors, and controls

the physical systems through actuators [37]. The supervisory control layer consists of historian databases, software application servers, Human-Machine Interface (HMI), and workstation. The historian databases and software application servers enable the efficient operation of the ICS. The low-level components are configured and monitored with the help of workstation and HMI, respectively [37].

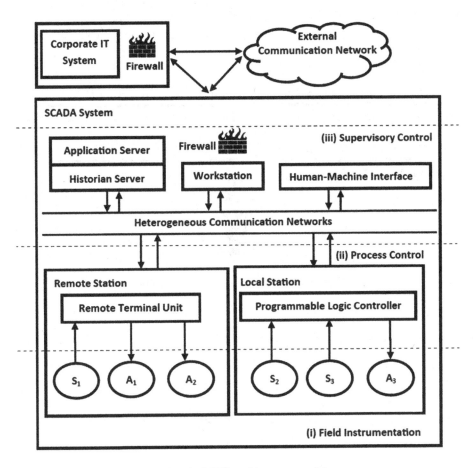

Fig. 3. Typical ICS architecture and layers

4.2   Case Study Overview

This case study overview is based on a site visit to a floodgate in the Netherlands. Some critical information has purposely been anonymised for security concerns. Figure 4 schematises a floodgate being primarily operated by Supervisory Control and Data Acquisition (SCADA) system along with an operations centre.

Figure 5 illustrates the SCADA architecture of the floodgate. The sensor (S_1) (which is located near the floodgate) is used to measure the water level. There is also a water level scale which is visible to the operator from the operations centre. The sensor measurements are then sent to the PLC. If the water level reaches the higher limit, PLC would send an alarm notification to the operator through the HMI, and the operator would need to close the floodgate in this case. The HMI would also provide information like the water level and the current state of the floodgate (open/close). The actuator opens/closes the floodgate. The data transmission used in this case is wired. Electricity is the only energy source in the operations centre.

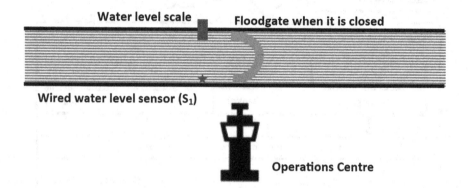

Fig. 4. Physical layout of the floodgate

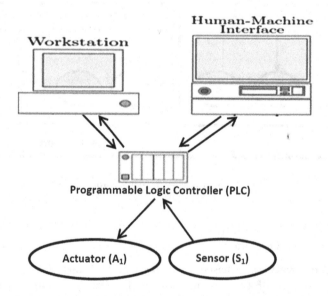

Fig. 5. SCADA architecture of the floodgate

5   Development and Application of the Methodology

In this section, we describe our framework with the type of variables and their relationships. Furthermore, we use an illustrative case of a floodgate in the Netherlands to explain how we combine BN and fishbone diagram to distinguish between (intentional) attacks and (accidental) technical failures.

5.1   Framework for Distinguishing Attacks and Technical Failures

The developed BN framework is grounded in BN models used for diagnostic purposes in different domains [6,16,32,33]. Studying the aforementioned diagnostic BN models in Sect. 2, we adopted and customised a set of variables to develop our BN framework. The type of variables which we adopted are: (i) risk factors [6,32], (ii) hypothesis [33], and (iii) observations (or test results) [16].

Pecchia et al. [33] used a hypothesis variable in their BN model as a classifier node to classify whether the user is compromised or not in shared computing infrastructures. We adopted the notion of a classifier node from Pecchia et al. [33] as it is the basis to the purposes of the present study. However, we defined it as the problem variable as it is an abnormal behavior in a component of the ICS (observable problem) in our work. For instance, the sensor (S_1) sends incorrect water level measurements. The purpose of the hypothesis variable in Pecchia et al. is to determine whether the user is compromised or not in sharing computing infrastructures, whereas in our work it is used to determine the major cause of the problem. An abnormal behavior in the technological components could be mainly caused by intentional attacks, accidental technical failures, human errors, or natural disasters [14]. However, the main objective of our study is to distinguish between attacks and technical failures. Therefore, we considered intentional attack and accidental technical failure as major causes of the problem. In addition, we introduced a category "others" in case the major cause of the problem is neither intentional attack nor accidental technical failure. For instance, the sensor (S_1) is misplaced in a different location by an operator. In this case, the major cause of the problem is human error and would thus be determined as "others".

Onisko et al. [32] and Curiac et al. [6] defined risk factors as the factors that would increase the likelihood of a disease. We, accordingly, adopted the term risk factors, and defined them as contributory factors since they contribute to the major cause of the problem in our work. For instance, "weak physical access-control" could contribute to the sensor (S_1) sending incorrect water level measurements due to an attack. Furthermore, there might be common contributory factors to different major causes of the problem. For instance, "outdated technology" could contribute to both the sensor (S_1) sending incorrect water level measurements due to an attack and a technical failure.

In general, observations (or test results) play an important role in diagnostics. Huang et al. [16] defined observations as any information useful for allocating the root causes such as those mentioned in the customer's reports or the outcomes of tests performed by diagnostic technicians. We defined observations (or test results) as any information useful for determining the major cause of the problem based on the outcomes of tests. For instance, the outcome of the test "whether the sensor (S_1) sends correct water level measurements after cleaning the sensor (S_1)?" would provide an additional information to determine the major cause (accidental technical failure) of the problem accurately. The observation (or test results) variables can be elicited from different sources such as experts, product manuals, and previous incident reports. For instance, the global water level sensor WL400 product manual lists troubleshooting tests for incorrect water level measurements due to (accidental) technical failures [12]. One of the troubleshooting tests listed in the product manual is to clean the sensor following the maintenance instructions and check whether the sensor sends correct water level measurements. Figure 6 shows the BN structure to build BN models for determining the major cause of an abnormal behavior in a component of the ICS, representing the causal relationship between the contributory factors, the problem, and the observations (or test results).

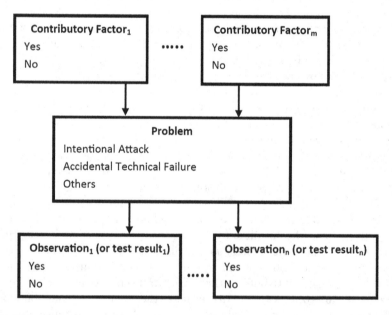

Fig. 6. BN structure to determine the major cause of an abnormal behavior in a component of the ICS

5.2   Combining Bayesian Networks and Fishbone Diagrams

Knowledge elicitation plays an important role to construct BN model especially with the appropriate variables for the considered problem [15, 34]. There are challenges to solely rely on BN for knowledge elicitation. For instance, BN is not easy-to-use for brainstorming with domain experts as it could be time-consuming to explain the notion of BN and also to change its structure instantly based on discussions during brainstorming sessions. Notably, expert knowledge is one of the predominant data sources utilised to build BN structure with appropriate variables especially in domains where there is a limited availability of data like cyber security [5]. Therefore, our framework would be incomplete without an effective method for knowledge elicitation.

In our work, fishbone diagram is used as the foundation to develop an effective method for knowledge elicitation especially based on their advantages stated in Sect. 3. Furthermore, there are additional benefits in the use of fishbone diagram in our work. We would mainly rely on experts from two different domains in addition to other sources for knowledge elicitation to construct BN models: (i) security, dealing with intentional attacks, and (ii) safety, dealing with accidental technical failures. In case we start building a BN model directly without utilising the fishbone diagram to elicit data from experts, it would be difficult to visualise which contributory factors and observations (or test results) corresponds to each major cause of the problem. This could make it difficult for the experts especially during brainstorming sessions. The fishbone diagram structure shows the potential to tackle this challenge. In some cases, there might be common contributory factors. For instance, "outdated technology" is a common contributory factor to two major causes of the problem (i.e., "outdated technology" could contribute to the sensor (S_1) sending incorrect water level measurements due to both "intentional attack" and "accidental technical failure"). If we start building a BN model directly without utilising the fishbone diagram to elicit data from experts, this could lead to duplication of common contributory factors using different terminologies in the BN.

In addition, BN structure is not easily changeable especially with a large number of contributory factors and observations (or test results) elicited from experts during brainstorming sessions. The fishbone diagram structure makes it easier to refine/update a large number of contributory factors and observations (or test results) instantly based on discussions during brainstorming sessions with experts. It would also help to visualise contributory factors and observations (or test results) from other sources such as literature and previous incidents. Finally, we can convert the constructed fishbone diagram into a corresponding BN model after the completion of knowledge elicitation to constitute the quantitative part of the corresponding BN model.

5.3   Extended Fishbone Diagrams and Translated BNs

We considered the example problem "sensor (S_1) sends incorrect water level measurements" as it could develop more complex situations in the case of floodgate.

In case the floodgate closes when it should not based on the incorrect water level measurements sent by the sensor (S_1), it would lead to severe economic damage, for instance, by delaying cargo ships. On the other hand, in case the floodgate opens when it should not due to incorrect water level measurements sent by the sensor (S_1), it would lead to flooding.

Figure 7 shows a fishbone diagram based on the example mentioned above. We considered "sensor (S_1) sends incorrect water level measurements" as the problem. Furthermore, we considered two major causes of the problem: intentional attack and accidental technical failure as mentioned earlier. These major causes of the problem would be the categories in our fishbone diagram. Finally, we mapped the appropriate contributory factors under each category. In this case, "outdated technology" is the common contributory factor that could contribute to sensor (S_1) sending incorrect water level measurements due to intentional attack and accidental technical failure. In this case, we listed "weak physical access-control" as one of the contributory factors in the category of intentional attack. This is because weak physical access-control could contribute to sensor (S_1) sending incorrect water level measurements due to an intentional attack.

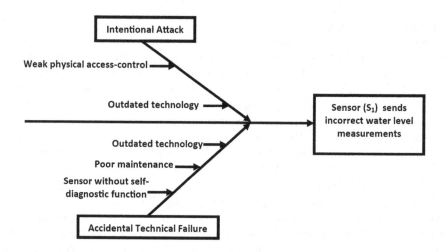

Fig. 7. Fishbone diagram example

Noticeably, fishbone diagrams do not consist of observations (or test results), which need to be elicited in our work. However, we could extend the fishbone diagram to incorporate observations (or test results) as shown in Fig. 8. This would allow us to elicit complete information needed to construct BN models especially with the three different types of variables and cause-effect relationships in our BN framework. The extended fishbone diagram is shown in Fig. 8 with an additional component: observations (or test results). The arrows in the fishbone diagram represent the causal relationship. The categories stated on the left side of the problem in the fishbone diagram are the major causes of the problem. Therefore, these categories has the arrows directing towards the problem which represent the causal relationship between the causes and the problem. However, the categories stated on the right side of the problem are used for reference to elicit observations (or test results) that would be useful for determining the particular major cause of the problem. Figure 9 shows the extended version of our fishbone diagram example with observations (or test results).

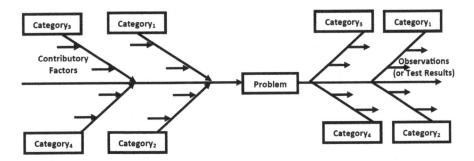

Fig. 8. Extended fishbone diagram structure

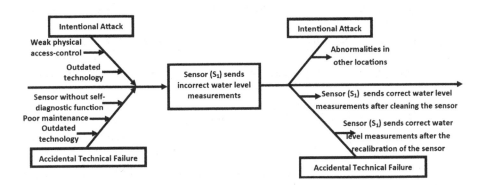

Fig. 9. Extended fishbone diagram example

Extended fishbone diagrams might look similar to qualitative bowtie diagrams, but, they are different. The observations (or test results) on the right side of the problem node in the extended fishbone diagram help distinguish between *different* events (intentional attack and accidental technical failure), Whereas bowtie diagrams are aimed at representing the possible consequences of a *fixed* event. Furthermore, qualitative bowties [36] consider recovery measures/reactive controls on the right side of the problem node. This is not relevant to our application because we focus on diagnostics. On the other hand, extended fishbone diagrams consider preventive controls/barriers implicitly on the left side of the problem node, as part of the contributory factors. For instance, "weak physical access-control for the sensor" is one of the contributory factors. The evidence supplied by the operator in the BN for this node would depend on the preventive controls/barriers that are in place. In case there are physical access-control measures implemented in that specific application, the operator would supply the evidence as 'No' for this node in the BN.

Once the fishbone diagram is developed, it should be translated to a BN based on the following steps:

i. The considered problem in the fishbone diagram is mapped to the problem variable in the middle layer of the BN as shown in Fig. 10.

ii. The categories used in the fishbone diagram would be states of the problem variable in our BN. In addition to these states, there would be an additional state "Others" in our BN. As mentioned in Sect. 5.1, this would be determined in case the major cause of the problem is neither intentional attack nor accidental technical failure.

iii. The elicited contributory factors in the fishbone diagram are mapped to the contributory factor variables in the upper layer of the BN as shown in Fig. 10. The contributory factors that correspond to both intentional attack and accidental technical failure in the fishbone diagram would be treated as a single contributory factor in the BN. For instance, "outdated technology" in our example would be treated as a single contributory factor in BN as shown in Fig. 10. However, the contributory factors that correspond to both intentional attack and accidental technical failure would be reflected through the conditional probabilities of "sensor (S_1) sends incorrect water level measurements". We considered the contributory factors as binary discrete variables based on their features. However, continuous variables could also have been used. We utilised the states *"Yes"* and *"No"* for our contributory factors as shown in Fig. 10.

iv. The elicited observations (or test results) in the fishbone diagram are mapped to the observations (or test results) in the lower layer of the BN as shown in Fig. 10. We considered the observations (or test results) as binary discrete variables based on their characteristics. We employed the states *"Yes"* and *"No"* for our observations (or test results) as shown in Fig. 10.

Once the fishbone diagram is translated to a corresponding BN model, the quantitative part of the BN should be populated. Due to limited data availability, expert knowledge is the predominant data source used to populate CPTs of BNs in cyber security [5]. In our work, we did not investigate whether fishbone diagrams could be used as a means to elicit probabilities from experts as our main objective is to elicit appropriate variables in the construction of the BN structure for the considered problem.

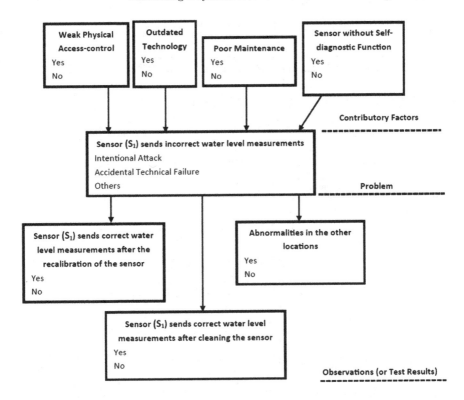

Fig. 10. Translated BN from fishbone diagram example

However, it is important to investigate whether fishbone diagrams could be used to elicit CPTs from experts in the future. The translated BN with illustrative priori marginal and conditional probabilities, representing the causal relationships between the contributory factors, the problem, and the observations (or test results), is shown in Fig. 11.

Once the quantitative part of the BN is populated, the BN could be used in practice for different scenarios and their probabilities could be updated based on evidences obtained. In the example shown in Fig. 11, we provided the evidence for the contributory factors "Weak Physical Access Control = Yes", "Outdated Technology = Yes", "Poor Maintenance = No" and "Sensor without Self-diagnostic Function = No", and observation (or test result) "Abnormalities in the other locations = Yes". Based on such evidence, the BN computes the posterior (updated) probabilities of the other nodes. The BN in Fig. 11 determines that the problem "Sensor (S1) sends incorrect water level measurements" is most likely due to (intentional) attack based on the evidence provided.

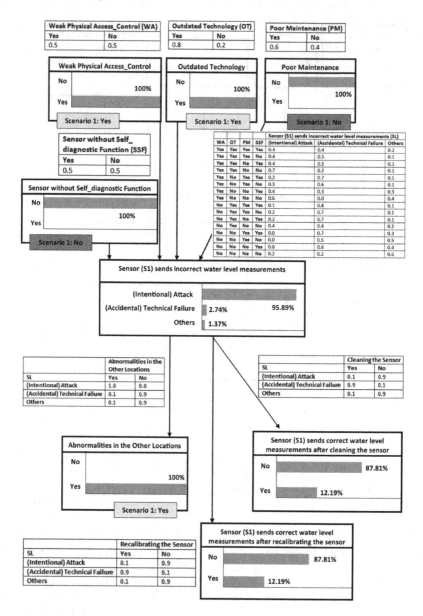

Fig. 11. Translated BN with updated probabilities based on the evidence

6   Conclusions and Future Work

Adequate decision support for distinguishing intentional attacks and accidental technical failures is missing. In this paper, we customised and utilised three different types of variables from existing diagnostic BN models in a BN framework to construct BN models for distinguishing intentional attacks and accidental technical failures. In our BN framework, the upper layer consists of contributory factors, the middle layer consists of a problem variable and the lower layer consists of observations (or test results). Furthermore, we extended and combined fishbone diagram with our BN framework to support knowledge elicitation from different sources. The important characteristics of our framework include: (i) it serves as a basis to provide decision support for responding to safety and security problems arise in the components of ICS, (ii) While determining the most likely cause of an abnormal behavior in a component of the ICS, it helps to consider both the contributory factors and observations (or test results) associated with it, and (iii) it facilitates knowledge elicitation especially from experts and its integration in BNs. Finally, we demonstrated the use of the developed methodology with an example problem "sensor (S_1) sends incorrect water level measurements" based on a case study in water management domain.

This work belongs to the broader theme of "Integrated safety and security". There are several studies within the sub-theme of "Integrated safety and security risk assessment" [4]. However, this work is associated with the sub-theme of "Integrated safety and security diagnostics", which mainly deals with the problem of distinguishing intentional attacks and accidental technical failures.

In the future, it would be useful to investigate whether fishbone diagrams could be used to elicit CPTs. The developed methodology would not be directly applicable when several problems arise at the same time. Therefore, it is important to address how fishbone diagrams could be used to elicit knowledge for those cases in the future and how it could be translated to a corresponding BN. Furthermore, we aim to evaluate our methodology based on applications in the water management domain.

Acknowledgements. This research received funding from the Netherlands Organisation for Scientific Research (NWO) in the framework of the Cyber Security research program under the project *"Secure Our Safety: Building Cyber Security for Flood Management (SOS4Flood)"*.

References

1. Asllani, A., Ali, A.: Securing information systems in airports: a practical approach. In: 2011 International Conference for Internet Technology and Secured Transactions (ICITST), pp. 314–318. IEEE (2011)
2. Ben-Gal, I., Ruggeri, F., Faltin, F., Kenett, R.: Bayesian networks. Encyclopedia of statistics in quality and reliability (2007)
3. Chen, G., Yu, H.: Bayesian network and its application in maize diseases diagnosis. In: Li, D. (ed.) CCTA 2007. TIFIP, vol. 259, pp. 917–924. Springer, Boston, MA (2008). https://doi.org/10.1007/978-0-387-77253-0_22
4. Chockalingam, S., Hadžiosmanović, D., Pieters, W., Teixeira, A., van Gelder, P.: Integrated safety and security risk assessment methods: a survey of key characteristics and applications. In: Havarneanu, G., Setola, R., Nassopoulos, H., Wolthusen, S. (eds.) CRITIS 2016. LNCS, vol. 10242, pp. 50–62. Springer, Cham (2017). https://doi.org/10.1007/978-3-319-71368-7_5

5. Chockalingam, S., Pieters, W., Teixeira, A., van Gelder, P.: Bayesian network models in cyber security: a systematic review. In: Lipmaa, H., Mitrokotsa, A., Matulevičius, R. (eds.) NordSec 2017. LNCS, vol. 10674, pp. 105–122. Springer, Cham (2017). https://doi.org/10.1007/978-3-319-70290-2_7

6. Curiac, D.I., Vasile, G., Banias, O., Volosencu, C., Albu, A.: Bayesian network model for diagnosis of psychiatric diseases. In: Proceedings of the ITI 2009 31st International Conference on Information Technology Interfaces, pp. 61–66. IEEE (2009)

7. Darwiche, A.: Bayesian networks. Found. Artif. Intell. **3**, 467–509 (2008)

8. Desai, M.S., Johnson, R.A.: Using a fishbone diagram to develop change management strategies to achieve first-year student persistence. SAM Adv. Manag. J. **78**(2), 51 (2013)

9. Doggett, A.M.: Root cause analysis: a framework for tool selection. Qual. Manag. J. **12**(4), 34–45 (2005)

10. Endi, M., Elhalwagy, Y., et al.: Three-layer PLC/SCADA system architecture in process automation and data monitoring. In: 2010 The 2nd International Conference on Computer and Automation Engineering (ICCAE), vol. 2, pp. 774–779. IEEE (2010)

11. Estabragh, Z.S., et al.: Bayesian network modeling for diagnosis of social anxiety using some cognitive-behavioral factors. Netw. Model. Anal. Health Inform. Bioinform. **2**(4), 257–265 (2013)

12. GlobalWater: Global water level sensor - wl400 product manual (2009). http://www.globalw.com/downloads/WL400/WL400manual.pdf

13. González-López, J., et al.: Development and validation of a Bayesian network for the differential diagnosis of anterior uveitis. Eye **30**(6), 865 (2016)

14. Grimvall, G., Holmgren, Å., Jacobsson, P., Thedéen, T.: Risks in Technological Systems. Springer, Heidelberg (2009). https://doi.org/10.1007/978-1-84882-641-0

15. Henrion, M.: Practical issues in constructing a Bayes' belief network. arXiv preprint arXiv:1304.2725 (2013)

16. Huang, Y., McMurran, R., Dhadyalla, G., Jones, R.P.: Probability based vehicle fault diagnosis: Bayesian network method. J. Intell. Manuf. **19**(3), 301–311 (2008)

17. Ilie, G., Ciocoiu, C.N.: Application of fishbone diagram to determine the risk of an event with multiple causes. Manag. Res. Pract. **2**(1), 1–20 (2010)

18. Ishikawa, K., Ishikawa, K.: Guide to Quality Control, vol. 2. Asian Productivity Organization, Tokyo (1982)

19. Jianhui, L., Zhang, J., Mingdi, J.: Application of BN in the fault diagnosis of brake failure system. Appl. Mech. Mater. **602–605**, 1684–1688 (2014)

20. Kahn Jr., C.E., Roberts, L.M., Shaffer, K.A., Haddawy, P.: Construction of a Bayesian network for mammographic diagnosis of breast cancer. Comput. Biol. Med. **27**(1), 19–29 (1997)

21. KasperskyLab: Five myths of industrial control systems security (2014). https://media.kaspersky.com/pdf/DataSheet_KESB_5Myths-ICSS_Eng_WEB.pdf

22. Kipersztok, O., Dildy, G.A.: Evidence-based Bayesian networks approach to airplane maintenance. In: Proceedings of the 2002 International Joint Conference on Neural Networks, IJCNN 2002, vol. 3, pp. 2887–2892. IEEE (2002)

23. Knowles, W., Prince, D., Hutchison, D., Disso, J.F.P., Jones, K.: A survey of cyber security management in industrial control systems. Int. J. Crit. Infrastruct. Prot. **9**, 52–80 (2015)

24. Korb, K.B., Nicholson, A.E.: Bayesian Artificial Intelligence. CRC Press, Boca Raton (2010)

25. Kwan, M., Chow, K.-P., Lai, P., Law, F., Tse, H.: Analysis of the digital evidence presented in the Yahoo! Case. In: Peterson, G., Shenoi, S. (eds.) DigitalForensics 2009. IAICT, vol. 306, pp. 241–252. Springer, Heidelberg (2009). https://doi.org/10.1007/978-3-642-04155-6_18

26. Kwan, M., Chow, K.-P., Law, F., Lai, P.: Reasoning about evidence using Bayesian networks. In: Ray, I., Shenoi, S. (eds.) DigitalForensics 2008. ITIFIP, vol. 285, pp. 275–289. Springer, Boston, MA (2008). https://doi.org/10.1007/978-0-387-84927-0_22

27. Luca, L., Stancioiu, A.: The study applying a quality management tool to identify the causes of a defect in an automotive. In: Proceedings of the 3rd International Conference on Automotive and Transport Systems (2012)

28. Macaulay, T., Singer, B.L.: Cybersecurity for Industrial Control Systems: SCADA, DCS, PLC, HMI, and SIS. Auerbach Publications, Boca Raton (2016)

29. Moreira, M.W., Rodrigues, J.J., Oliveira, A.M., Ramos, R.F., Saleem, K.: A preeclampsia diagnosis approach using Bayesian networks. In: 2016 IEEE International Conference on Communications (ICC), pp. 1–5. IEEE (2016)

30. Nakatsu, R.T.: Reasoning with Diagrams: Decision-Making and Problem-Solving with Diagrams. Wiley, Hoboken (2009)

31. Nikovski, D.: Constructing bayesian networks for medical diagnosis from incomplete and partially correct statistics. IEEE Trans. Knowl. Data Eng. 9(4), 509–516 (2000)

32. Oniśko, A., Druzdzel, M.J., Wasyluk, H.: Extension of the Hepar II model to multiple-disorder diagnosis. In: Kłopotek, M., Michalewicz, M., Wierzchoń, S.T. (eds.) Intelligent Information Systems, pp. 303–313. Springer, Heidelberg (2000). https://doi.org/10.1007/978-3-7908-1846-8_27

33. Pecchia, A., Sharma, A., Kalbarczyk, Z., Cotroneo, D., Iyer, R.K.: Identifying compromised users in shared computing infrastructures: a data-driven Bayesian network approach. In: 2011 30th IEEE International Symposium on Reliable Distributed Systems, pp. 127–136. IEEE (2011)

34. Przytula, K.W., Thompson, D.: Construction of Bayesian networks for diagnostics. In: 2000 IEEE Aerospace Conference Proceedings, vol. 5, pp. 193–200. IEEE (2000)

35. RISI: German steel mill cyber attack (2018). http://www.risidata.com/database/detail/german-steel-mill-cyber-attack

36. de Ruijter, A., Guldenmund, F.: The bowtie method: a review. Saf. Sci. 88, 211–218 (2016)

37. Skopik, F., Smith, P.D.: Smart Grid Security: Innovative Solutions for a Modernized Grid. Syngress, Boston (2015)

38. Wang, J.A., Guo, M.: Vulnerability categorization using Bayesian networks. In: Proceedings of the Sixth Annual Workshop on Cyber Security and Information Intelligence Research, p. 29. ACM (2010)

39. Wang, X.H., Zheng, B., Good, W.F., King, J.L., Chang, Y.H.: Computer-assisted diagnosis of breast cancer using a data-driven Bayesian belief network. Int. J. Med. Inform. 54(2), 115–126 (1999)

40. White, A.A., et al.: Cause-and-effect analysis of risk management files to assess patient care in the emergency department. Acad. Emerg. Med. 11(10), 1035–1041 (2004)

41. Zhao, C.H., Zhang, J., Zhong, X.Y., Zeng, J., Chen, S.J.: Analysis of accident safety risk of tower crane based on fishbone diagram and the analytic hierarchy process. In: Applied Mechanics and Materials. vol. 127, pp. 139–143. Trans Tech Publications (2012)
42. Zhu, Y., Qian, X.M., Liu, Z.Y., Huang, P., Yuan, M.Q.: Analysis and assessment of the Qingdao crude oil vapor explosion accident: lessons learnt. J. Loss Prev. Process. Ind. **33**, 289–303 (2015)

Disclosure Analysis of SQL Workflows

Marlon Dumas[1], Luciano García-Bañuelos[1(✉)], and Peeter Laud[2]

[1] University of Tartu, Tartu, Estonia
{marlon.dumas,luciano.garcia}@ut.ee
[2] Cybernetica, Tartu, Estonia
peeter.laud@cyber.ee

Abstract. In the context of business process management, the implementation of data minimization requirements requires that analysts are able to assert what private data each worker is able to access, not only directly via the inputs of the tasks they perform in a business process, but also indirectly via the chain of tasks that lead to the production of these inputs. In this setting, this paper presents a technique which, given a workflow that transforms a set of input tables into a set of output tables via a set of inter-related SQL statements, determines what information from each input table is disclosed by each output table, and under what conditions this disclosure occurs. The result of this disclosure analysis is a summary representation of the possible computations leading from the inputs of the workflow to a given output thereof.

1 Introduction

Data minimization is one of the principles underpinning the European General Data Protection Regulation (GDPR) as well as previous privacy frameworks and standards such as ISO 29100 [3]. In the context of Business Process Management (BPM) this principle entails that workers, contractors, and other stakeholders involved in the execution of a business process, should only have access to private data to the extent it is required to perform the tasks for which they are responsible. In order to verify compliance vis-a-vis of this requirement, analysts need to have a fine-grained understanding of what private data each worker is able to access, not only directly via the inputs of the tasks they perform, but also indirectly via the chain of tasks that lead to the production of these inputs.

Previous work on business process privacy analysis [1] has led to techniques for boolean ("yes-no") disclosure analysis. These techniques allow an analyst to determine whether or not a given stakeholder has access to a data object or data collection (e.g. a document or a database table). However, it does not allow analysts to determine what part of the data collection (e.g. what attributes) are accessible to each stakeholder and under which conditions.

This paper proposes a finer-grained disclosure analysis technique which characterizes how the contents of the database on top of which a business process is executed, affects each output of the process, specifically, which columns of

© Springer Nature Switzerland AG 2019
G. Cybenko et al. (Eds.): GraMSec 2018, LNCS 11086, pp. 51–70, 2019.
https://doi.org/10.1007/978-3-030-15465-3_4

which tables become part of an output, in which manner, and under which conditions. The proposed technique tasks as input a *SQL workflow*, which we define as a process model in the standard BPMN notation[1] in which each task corresponds to a SQL statement executed against a database. Each SQL statement in the workflow queries a set of input tables from the database and produces new tables, which can be later used by subsequent tasks in the workflow. The table (or set of tables) that are taken as input by the first SQL statements in the workflow are called the inputs. Conversely, the tables produced by the last SQL statements in the workflow are called the final output(s), while the tables produced by intermediate tasks in the workflow are called intermediate outputs.

As a running example, Fig. 1 presents an example SQL workflow from an Aid Distribution process, in which a country facing a catastrophe, requests aid from the international community. The situation requires distributing goods to the population via maritime transportation. Henceforth, a SQL workflow is executed to identify ships in nearby locations and to allocate berths to ships, such that ships can move people and goods from/to the requesting country.

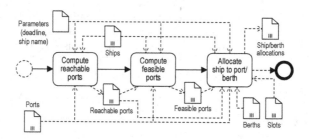

Fig. 1. Conceptual model of the *Aid distribution* scenario

Some of the inputs used in this workflow are confidential (e.g. ship location and capacities) and the countries involved in the process seek to minimize their exposure to different stakeholders. Accordingly, an analyst needs to determine: (i) who gets access to which input tables during the performance of the process? (ii) what information (e.g. table columns or functions over columns) are disclosed? and (iii) under what conditions this disclosure occurs? The disclosure analysis technique proposed in this paper supports this task by determining what information is disclosed via each intermediate and final output of the workflow, and under which conditions (i.e. for which table rows) this disclosure occurs.

The rest of the paper is structured as follows. Section 2 formalizes the notion of SQL workflow. Section 3 presents the disclosure analysis technique, while Sect. 4 presents how the output of this technique can be simplified and visually presented. Section 5 discusses related work, while Sect. 6 draws conclusions.

---

[1] http://www.bpmn.org/.

2   SQL Workflows

For the disclosure analysis, we assume that the overall computation is specified as
a set of inter-related SQL statements over a database. Each step takes some input
tables and derives new information that is stored in output tables which might
be used by subsequent steps. Each task in the SQL workflow is associated with
a SQL statement. Listing 1.1 presents the script associated with task "Compute
reachable ports" from the running example.

Listing 1.1. SQL script associated with task "Compute reachable ports"

```
1   create function earliest_arrival(
2     ship_latitude double, ship_longitude double,
3     port_latitude double, port_longitude double,
4     max_speed bigint) returns bigint as
5   $$
6   select ceil((point(ship_latitude, ship_longitude)
7                 <@> point(port_latitude, port_longitude)) / max_speed)::bigint
8   $$
9   language SQL immutable returns null on null input;
10
11  select port.port_id as port_id,
12    earliest_arrival(ship.longitude, ship.latitude, port.longitude,
13                      port.latitude, ship.maxspeed) as arrival
14  into reachable_ports
15  from ports as port, ships as ship, parameters as p
16  where earliest_arrival(ship.longitude, ship.latitude,
17            port.longitude, port.latitude, ship.maxspeed) <= p.deadline
18    and ship.name = p.shipname
19    and port.port_id = port.port_id;
```

The syntax used in the script is that of PostgreSQL and, as it can be seen, the
underlying query is not trivial. In this example, the script includes a user defined
function (i.e. `earliest_arrival`) that computes the time for a ship to reach
a port given their coordinates and the ship's speed. Each task can be associated
with any number of user-defined functions and at least one *select-into* statement
that would store the outcome of the computation on a (temporary) table, to
be consistent with the intent specified in the conceptual model. In Listing 1.1,
such *select-into* statement is defined in lines 11–19. Moreover, it can be seen
that such statement takes as input tables `ports`, `ships` and `parameters`
(highlighted in line 15) and stores the result in table `reachable_ports` (line
14), consistent with the model. The select statement, in turn, calls the function
`earliest_arrival` in lines 12 and 16, which is defined in lines 1–9.

SQL workflows may include sophisticated constructs to captures conditional
branching and concurrency, as per the BPMN standard. For simplicity, the disclosure analysis is performed not on the whole SQL workflow but on the set
of the runs of it. A run is the set nodes and edges that are visited on a SQL
workflow to track one possible execution of the workflow.

To illustrate the concept of run, consider the sample workflow in Fig. 2, which
contains AND gateways (cf. diamonds decorated with +) and XOR gateways (cf.
decorated with ×). The semantics of such gateways, as defined in the BPMN
specification [8], is the following. An AND gateway activates all the elements on
the outgoing paths and synchronizes the completion of all the elements on the

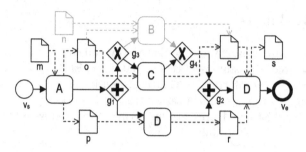

Fig. 2. Sample SQL workflow and its runs

incoming paths. Conversely, a XOR gateway activates only one outgoing path (cf. based on a predicated associated with the edge) or waits for the completion of one of the incoming paths. Henceforth, a run of this workflow is a connected subgraph of the process model that contains the start (entry) and the end (exit) node, and such that at most one outgoing edge of each XOR-split is represented. In the example shown in Fig. 2, there are exactly two runs, one of which is highlighted.

Before describing the method, we need to introduce some notation. Conceptually, a SQL workflow can be represented as a directed graph, formally defined as tuple $\mathcal{W} = (\mathcal{V}, \mathcal{E}, \mathcal{P}, \mathcal{O}, \mathcal{F}, \mathcal{V}^\times, \mathcal{V}^+, \mathcal{A}^D, \mathcal{A}^Q)$. There, $\mathcal{V}$ is the set of nodes and $\mathcal{E} \subseteq \mathcal{V} \times \mathcal{V}$ the set of control flow edges. For convenience, we assume that $\mathcal{V} = \mathcal{P} \cup \mathcal{V}^\times \cup \mathcal{V}^+ \cup \{v_s\} \cup \mathcal{V}_e$, where $\mathcal{P}$ denotes the set of data processing nodes, $\mathcal{G}^\times$ the set of AND gateways, $\mathcal{V}^+$ XOR gateways, v_s is the start node, and $\mathcal{V}_e$ is a non-empty set of end nodes (e.g. v_e). A SQL workflow must have exactly one start node and at least one end node. $\mathcal{O}$ is the set of data objects and $\mathcal{F} \subseteq (\mathcal{O} \times \mathcal{P}) \cup (\mathcal{P} \times \mathcal{O})$ the set of dataflow edges. Similarly, $\mathcal{A}^D : \mathcal{O} \to SQL$ is a mapping that associates data objects with SQL data definition statements, and $\mathcal{A}^Q : \mathcal{P} \to SQL$ a mapping that associates processing nodes with SQL data manipulation statements. Finally, we will write $\bullet v = \{v' \in \mathcal{V} | (v', v) \in \mathcal{E}\}$ to denote the set of predecessors of node v and $v\bullet = \{v' \in \mathcal{V} | (v, v') \in \mathcal{E}\}$ to refer to the set of successors of v.

Consider the workflow $\mathcal{W}$. We write $P(\mathcal{W})$ to denote the set of all runs of $\mathcal{W}$, iff for every $\rho \in P(\mathcal{W})$ with $\rho = (\mathcal{V}', \mathcal{E}')$, all the following conditions hold: (i) ρ is subgraph of $\mathcal{W}$, i.e. $\mathcal{V}' \subseteq \mathcal{V}$ and $\mathcal{E}' = \mathcal{E} \cap (\mathcal{V}' \times \mathcal{V}')$, (ii) ρ includes start/end nodes of $\mathcal{W}$, i.e. $v_s, v_e \in \mathcal{V}'$, (iii) ρ includes exactly one path incoming/outgoing XOR gateways, i.e. $\forall g \in \mathcal{V}' \cap \mathcal{V}^\times : | \bullet g \cap \mathcal{V}'| = |g \bullet \cap \mathcal{V}'| = 1$, (iv) ρ includes all paths incoming/outgoing nodes other than XOR gateways, i.e. $\forall g \in \mathcal{V}' \setminus \mathcal{V}^\times : \bullet g \subset \mathcal{V}' \wedge g\bullet \subset \mathcal{V}'$, and (v) all the nodes in ρ are in a path from the start node and finishes in at least one of end node v_e, i.e. $\forall v \in \mathcal{V}', \exists v_e \in \mathcal{V}_e : (v_s, v), (v, v_e) \in \mathcal{E}'^*$. The set $P(\mathcal{W})$ can be trivially computed if $\mathcal{W}$ is acyclic, using a tailored depth-first search traversal as presented in [9]. When the input SQL workflow contains loops, it is possible to unroll all the loops one iteration. The method described here can then be applied on the resulting acyclic workflow.

Note that the notion of a run is defined over the control flow edges of the input workflow. However, the data dependencies can be trivially derived for each run ρ by computing the subgraph over dataflow nodes (i.e. data objects) and edges induced by the set of data processing nodes of ρ. Formally, $\mathcal{O}(\rho) \subset \mathcal{O}$ denotes the set of data objects associated with run ρ and is defined as $\mathcal{O}(\rho) = \{o \in \mathcal{O} | \exists v \in \mathcal{V}' : (v, d) \in \mathcal{E}' \vee (d, v) \in \mathcal{E}'\}$.

Finally, given a run ρ of a SQL workflow $\mathcal{W}$, we would need to derive the SQL script that the run would execute. Such a script can be derived from the SQL statements associated with data objects and data processing nodes, by concatenating them following a topological order of the nodes in the run. It is this script that serves as input to the disclosure analysis described below.

3   Disclosure Analysis

3.1   Databases, Schemas, and Queries

Workflow runs (cf. previous section) can be straightforwardly turned to *relational algebra workflows*. These workflows carry the same information, without the syntactic baggage of SQL. These workflows are defined in Fig. 3, also depending on the definitions of relation and database schemas, as stated below.

A *relation schema* is $r(a_1 : D_1, \ldots, a_n : D_n; \mathsf{Dis}_r)$, where r is relation name, $a_1, \ldots, a_n$ are attribute names, $D_1, \ldots, D_n$ are sets, and Dis_r is a set of subsets of the set of attributes $\{a_1, \ldots, a_n\}$. The last component indicates, which attributes or sets of them must be unique in a relation satisfying this schema. An element of Dis_r describes a possible index for a table satisfying the relation schema r. In our analysis, we require Dis_r to contain at least one set of attributes.

Let $D[r]$ denote the set $D_1 \times \cdots \times D_n$. A relation R over the schema r is a subset of $D[r]$, such that for each $\{a_{i_1}, \ldots, a_{i_k}\} \in \mathsf{Dis}_r$ and each $(x_{i_1}, \ldots, x_{i_k}) \in D_{i_1} \times \cdots \times D_{i_k}$ there is at most one $(y_1, \ldots, y_n) \in R$ satisfying $y_{i_1} = x_{i_1}, \ldots, y_{i_k} = x_{i_k}$. Let $\mathcal{X}_r$ denote the set of all relations over the schema r. For $x \in D[r]$, let $x[a_i]$ denote the value of attribute a_i on x.

A *database schema* is $dbs = (t_1 : r_1, \ldots, t_m : r_m)$, where $t_1, \ldots, t_m$ are *table names* and $r_1, \ldots, r_m$ are relation schemas. A database over the schema is a tuple of relations $\mathbf{D} = (R_1, \ldots, R_m)$, where R_i is over r_i. For a fixed dbs, let $\mathcal{Y}$ denote the set of all databases over the schema dbs, and let $D[t_i]$ denote the set $D[r_i]$. For a database $Y \in \mathcal{Y}$, let $Y.t_i \subseteq D[r]$ denote its table t_i.

Suppose that we have selected the primary keys for each table in the database. That means, for each $t : r$ in the database schema, we have selected $\mathsf{index}_r \in \mathsf{Dis}_r$. We can then think of a relation R over the schema $r(a_1 : D_1, \ldots, a_n : D_n; \mathsf{Dis}_r)$ as a set of partial functions $\mathsf{f}_1^r, \ldots, \mathsf{f}_n^r$ from the cartesian product $\prod_{a_i \in \mathsf{index}_r} D_i$ to each of the sets $D_1, \ldots, D_n$. All these partial functions are defined on the same domain. If $a_i \in \mathsf{index}_r$, then the function f_i^r must be a partial projection.

The syntax for workflows of simple database queries is given in Fig. 3. The workflow is executed against a database with a certain schema dbs. The meaning of the syntax for queries Q is the following.

$$
\begin{aligned}
Q &::= t & &| \; Q_1 \times \cdots \times Q_k \; | \; [Q]_{a \to a'} & &| \; \sigma(Q; e) \\
&\quad | \; \pi_{a_1, \ldots, a_k}(Q) \; | \; \mathsf{col}_{a \leftarrow e}(Q) & &| \; \mathsf{let} \; t = Q_1 \; \mathsf{in} \; Q_2 & &| \; Q_1 \cup Q_2 \\
&\quad | \; Q_1 \cap Q_2 & &| \; Q_1 \ltimes_e Q_2 & &| \; \mathsf{group}^{a_1, \ldots, a_k}_{(a'_1, \otimes_1), \ldots, (a'_l, \otimes_l)}(Q) \\
e &::= a & &| \; \otimes(e_1, \ldots, e_k)
\end{aligned}
$$

Fig. 3. Syntax of queries

- The query t returns the table t. This table must exist in the current database.
- The query $Q_1 \times \cdots \times Q_k$ returns the cartesian product of the results of queries $Q_1, \ldots, Q_k$. We require that the names of the attributes in $Q_1 \times \cdots \times Q_k$ are unique, i.e. the queries $Q_1, \ldots, Q_k$ result in datasets which have non-intersecting sets of attributes.
- $[Q]_{a \to a'}$ executes the query Q. Its result is a relation with a certain schema; this schema must contain attribute a, which is then renamed to a'.
- $\sigma(Q; e)$ filters the result of the query Q with the expression e. The expression e, which must return a Boolean value, is built up from attributes and arithmetic/relational/logical etc. operations $\otimes$. We expect the expressions e to be well-typed, but will not discuss this here any more.
- $\pi_{a_1, \ldots, a_k}(Q)$ projects the result of Q onto attributes $a_1, \ldots, a_k$. The dataset returned by Q must have these attributes in its schema.
- $\mathsf{col}_{a \leftarrow e}(Q)$ runs Q and then adds a new column (a new attribute) to the result. The name of the attribute is a. Its value for each row is computed from the existing attributes of this row according to the expression e.
- $\mathsf{let} \; t = Q_1 \; \mathsf{in} \; Q_2$ is used to build workflows. It executes the query Q_1 against the current and gives the resulting dataset the name t. It will then execute the query Q_2 against the database the contains the current database, as well as the the table t.
- $Q_1 \cup Q_2$ and $Q_1 \cap Q_2$ return the union and the intersection of the results of Q_1 and Q_2, which must have the same schema.
- $Q_1 \ltimes_e Q_2$ returns all such rows $\mathbf{r}_1$ from the result of Q_1, such that there exists no row $\mathbf{r}_2$ in the result of Q_2, such that the boolean expression e holds. This construction is used to build outer joins.
- $\mathsf{group}^{a_1, \ldots, a_k}_{(a'_1, \otimes_1), \ldots, (a'_l, \otimes_l)}(Q)$ expresses grouping and aggregation of the result of Q. The resulting dataset will have attributes $a_1, \ldots, a_k, a'_1, \ldots, a'_l$, with $\{a_1, \ldots, a_k\}$ forming the index. There will be a row with particular values of $a_1, \ldots, a_k$ if the result of Q had at least one row with these values. The attribute a'_i in the query result will be the aggregation by $\otimes_i$ of the attributes a'_i in all these rows in the result of Q.

Figure 3 gives us a rich language for expressing SQL workflows, allowing the use of various types of filters, joins, and projections. Note that the ORDER BY component of a SQL statement does not change the resulting relation, hence sorting does not appear among our relational algebra operations. However, sorting may be combined with the row_number() function that exists in some SQL dialects. More generally, the row number generation can be done after the dataset has been partitioned according to the values of some other column(s). The row numbers of sorted datasets have been used in the last step of the scenario depicted in Fig. 1. Such use of ordering and row numbers can be modelled with the help of grouping and aggregation.

3.2 Dependency Graphs and Summaries

A *dependency graph* (DG) is a directed graph $G = (V, E, \mathsf{s}, \mathsf{t}, \ldots)$, where $\mathsf{s}, \mathsf{t} : E \rightarrow V$ give the source and the target nodes of arcs. The DG also has the following additional components:

- There are subsets of nodes $I, O \subseteq V$. The in-degree of any node in I and the out-degree of any node in O is 0. The in-degree of any node in O is 1. These nodes represent the inputs coming to, and the outputs produced by the DG.
- There is a set **Op** of possible operations. Each *internal* node v (i.e. $v \in V \backslash (I \cup O)$) has a label $\lambda(v) \in$ **Op**.
- For each internal node v, its incoming arcs are linearly ordered; let $<_v$ denote the ordering relation. The number of incoming arcs of an internal node v is equal to the number of operands that the operation $\lambda(v)$ expects.

Let **V** be a set of values; the operations in **Op** consume and produce values. Given the semantics $[\![\otimes]\!] : \mathbf{V}^* \rightarrow \mathbf{V}$ of each operation $\otimes \in$ **Op**, the dependency graph G defines a mapping $[\![G]\!] : \mathbf{V}^I \rightarrow \mathbf{V}^O$. If G has no directed cycles, then this mapping is defined by assigning a value to each node of G, with the values for input nodes given by the input to $[\![G]\!]$; the values of intermediate nodes v computed by applying $\lambda(v)$ to the values of direct ancestors of v; and the values of output nodes being equal to the values of their direct ancestors. For dependency graphs with directed cycles, the semantics can be defined using a fix-point construction [11], if there is a partial order on **V** with the least element $\bot$, and if the operations are monotonic. In this deliverable, we do not have cyclic dependency graphs, hence we will not discuss this any more.

A dependency graph may be infinite, with infinitely many inputs and outputs, as well as with nodes having an infinite number of incoming edges. In the latter case, the operation in the node must make sense for infinite number of inputs (e.g. it may be conjunction or disjunction of booleans). If G is infinite then $[\![G]\!]$ is still well-defined as long as for each output node v_O there is a bound B_O, such that any path in the graph ending in v_O has length at most B_O.

The computations of an SQL workflow can naturally be expressed as infinite dependency graphs. Given a table t with the schema $r(a_1 : D_1, \ldots, a_n : D_n)$ and its index index_r, we express its use in a workflow by the input nodes $v_{i,K}^t$ for each attribute a_i and each possible value K of the index attributes of t. Additionally, the use of the table t is expressed by the input nodes $v_{\exists,K}^t$, denoting whether the row with the index value K is present in the database. As the index attributes typically come from infinite sets (e.g. integers), there are infinitely many possible values K. The input nodes $v_{i,K}^t$ and $v_{\exists,K}^t$ are followed by computation nodes for the expressions e occurring in the workflow. Again, these are replicated as many times as there are possible values for index attributes in the relations that they work on. We end up with a graph with output nodes $w_{j,K'}$ and $w_{\exists,K'}$ for each possible value K' of the index of the resulting dataset. The attributes of the index of the resulting dataset, and hence also the set from which the values K' come from, can be computed from the query as shown in Fig. 4.

Q	index_Q
t	$\prod_{a_i \in \text{index}_r} D_i$, where $r(a_1 : D_1, \ldots, a_n : D_n)$ is the schema of t
$Q_1 \times \cdots \times Q_k$	$\text{index}_{Q_1} \times \cdots \times \text{index}_{Q_k}$
$[Q]_{a \to a'}$	index_Q
$\sigma(Q; e)$	index_Q
$\pi_{a_1, \ldots, a_k}(Q)$	index_Q
$\text{col}_{a \leftarrow e}(Q)$	index_Q
let $t = Q_1$ in Q_2	index_{Q_2}, where $\text{index}_t \leftarrow \text{index}_{Q_1}$

Fig. 4. Computing the index set of the query

We represent the infinite dependency graphs as finite summaries. The summary dependency graph (SDG) has the same components $(V, E, I, O, \lambda, <)$ as a DG. However, there is additional structure for the nodes and the edges.

- There is a set of possible index sets $\mathcal{S}$. The elements of $\mathcal{S}$ are typically the set of integers, the set of strings, the unit set (a set with a single element). For handling a particular database schema, $\mathcal{S}$ must contain all sets D_i that are associated to some attribute in the index of some table in this schema.
- Each node $v \in V$ has the *dimension* $\dim(v)$ and *input dimension* $\overrightarrow{\dim}(v)$. They are both sets.
  - In our representation, both $\dim(v)$ and $\overrightarrow{\dim}(v)$ are sets that can be expressed as *polynomials* over $\mathcal{S}$. A polynomial over a set of sets $\mathcal{X}$ is a set of the form $\sum_{i=1}^{n} \prod_{j=1}^{m_i} X_{ij}$, where $X_{ij} \in \mathcal{X}$, and $\sum$ denotes the non-intersecting union (or: sum) of sets. Hence there is a finite representation for $\dim(v)$ and $\overrightarrow{\dim}(v)$.
- Each node v has a mapping $\delta(v)$ from $\overrightarrow{\dim}(v)$ to $\dim(v)$.
  - In our representation, the mapping $\delta(v)$ is a *canonical polynomial map*. Let $\overrightarrow{\dim}(v) = \sum_{i=1}^{n} \prod_{j=1}^{m_i} X_{ij}$ and $\dim(v) = \sum_{i=1}^{s} \prod_{j=1}^{t_i} Y_{ij}$. A canonical polynomial map is built up from identity mappings between X_{ij} and $Y_{i'j'}$ (which must be the same set) as follows:
    * A canonical mapping $c : \prod_{j=1}^{m} X_j \to \prod_{j=1}^{t} Y_j$ is defined by an injective mapping $\gamma : \{1, \ldots, t\} \to \{1, \ldots, m\}$ satisfying $X_{\gamma(j)} = Y_j$ for all $j \in \{1, \ldots, t\}$. The mapping c is given by
      $$c(x_1, \ldots, x_m) = (x_{\gamma^{-1}(1)}, \ldots, x_{\gamma^{-1}(t)}).$$
    * A canonical mapping from $\prod_{j=1}^{m} X_j$ to $\sum_{i=1}^{s} \prod_{j=1}^{t_i} Y_{ij}$ consists of an index $q \in \{1, \ldots, s\}$ and a canonical mapping of the previous kind from $\prod_{j=1}^{m} X_j$ to $\prod_{j=1}^{t_q} Y_{qj}$.

* A canonical mapping from $\sum_{i=1}^{n} \prod_{j=1}^{m_i} X_{ij}$ to $\sum_{i=1}^{s} \prod_{j=1}^{t_i} Y_{ij}$ consists of n canonical mappings of the previous kind.
- If $\delta(v)$ is not the identity mapping, then the node v must have exactly one incoming arc.
- Each arc $\alpha \in E$ still has a single target node $\mathsf{t}(\alpha)$. But an arc may have several source nodes, i.e. $\mathsf{s}(\alpha) \subseteq V$.
- Each arc $\alpha \in E$ has a mapping $\overline{\delta}(\alpha)$ from $\overrightarrow{\dim}(\mathsf{t}(\alpha))$ to $\sum_{v \in \mathsf{s}(\alpha)} \dim(v)$.
  - Mapping $\overline{\delta}(\alpha)$ is again a canonical polynomial map.

A summary dependency graph G_{sum} is expanded to a potentially infinite dependency graph $G = \mathsf{expand}(G_{\mathrm{sum}})$ in the following manner:

- For each node v in the summary dependency graph, there are nodes $\{(v, x) \mid x \in \dim(v)\}$ in the actual dependency graph, which have the same operation $\lambda(v)$.
  - We call the node (v, x) in the actual dependency graph the *instance* x of the node v in the SDG.
- For each arc α going to a vertex v in the summary dependency graph, and for each element $x \in \overrightarrow{\dim}(v)$, there is an edge from the node $\overline{\delta}(\alpha)(x)$ to the node $\delta(v)(x)$. Note that the output of $\overline{\delta}(\alpha)(x)$ is a pair of some node $w \in \mathsf{s}(\alpha)$ and a value $y \in \dim(w)$.
  - Let $x \in \dim(v)$. If $\delta(v)$ is the identity mapping and thus $v \in G_{\mathrm{sum}}$ may have several input arcs, the ordering $<_{(v,x)}$ of the inputs of the vertex $(v, x) \in G$ is inherited from v. The vertex (v, x) has the same number of input arcs as the vertex v does.
  - Otherwise, the vertices $(v, x) \in G$ may have any number of inputs, perhaps an infinite number. In this case, $\lambda(v)$ must be an associative and commutative operation, and make sense for infinite number of inputs.

In our analysis, we translate an SQL workflow into a summary dependency graph. The semantics of a summary dependency graph is the same as the semantics of the dependency graph resulting from its expansion. This semantics can be related to the semantics of the SQL workflow in a manner that shows their equivalence. We simplify the summary dependency graph, removing spurious dependencies, while changing the semantics of the graph only in a manner that still relates it to the SQL workflow. From the resulting graph, we can read out the actual dependencies of each output, including the actual computation, as well as the conditions of outputting them.

The translation of a query Q to a summary dependency graph works in syntax-directed manner. We first translate the database schema, resulting in a Partial Summary Dependency Graph (PSDG) consisting of only input nodes. Beside the PSDG, we also get a mapping from the attributes of tables to the nodes. This PSDG is given as the input to the translation of Q. The result is another PSDG, which is post-processed to add the output nodes. The translation is given in Appendix A. Figure 5 shows the result of translating the workflow consisting of Listing 1.1, followed by the query into a SDG. We have removed dead nodes, and identity nodes from this figure. In this figure, the rectangles with sharp corners denote the nodes of SDG. In the top row, it lists the name of the operation and the ID of the node v. The following rows list the components of $\dim(v)$, these components are elements of $\mathcal{S}$. An arc α, where $\overline{\delta}(\alpha)$ is the identity mapping, is depicted as line ending in an arrow, possibly with a short label in the middle, indicating the position of the value flowing along this arc in the operation at $t(\alpha)$. If $\overline{\delta}(\alpha)$ is not identity, then it is depicted inside a rectangle with rounded corners. At the top of this rectangle is the label of the arc (if any), and other rows show, which dimension components of the target node correspond to which dimension components of the source node.

```
1  select rport.port_id, port.name,
2    earliest_arrival(ship.longitude, ship.latitude, port.longitude,
3                     port.latitude, ship.maxspeed) as arrival
4  from reachable_ports as rport, port, ship, parameters as p
5  where port.port_id = rport.port_id
6    and ship.name = p.shipname
```

4 Simplifications and Output Presentation

4.1 Simplifying the SDG

We have implemented a number of simplifications of SDG, both structural and semantical. Below we discuss these simplifications on the basis of the full scenario depicted in Fig. 1. A simplification operation, applied to a certain node or a group of nodes, checks whether the local context of these nodes matches some pattern. If it does, then these nodes are replaced with some other nodes that have the same effect semantically (or an effect that is similar in the view of our task to find which inputs end up where, how, and when), but have simpler structure.

The SDG is a very helpful data structure in determining the applicability of simplifications. The applicability of many simplifications can be determined locally, i.e. by considering a subgraph of bounded diameter. Also, more complex structural transformations have applicability checks which consist of simple traversals of the graph. Hence the current set of simplifications may be easily extended, depending on the needs of analysed scenarios.

One simplification may enable others. We thus run the simplifications in the order that seems to make the most sense; some simplifications (e.g. the removal of dead nodes) are run many times. In the following, we will describe some simplifications that our analyzer currently runs.

Removal of dead nodes. A node that has no descendants may be removed, unless it is an output node. Running this removal many times, we will remove all nodes that are not backwards reachable from any output node.

Folding of identity operations. An ID node (the node whose operation is identity; our translation from relational algebra expressions, given in Appendix A, produces many such nodes) can be cut out of paths: if v is an ID node and α is the arc leading to it, and β is any arc with the source v, then β may be replaced with the arc $\beta \circ \alpha$: we define $s(\beta \circ \alpha) = s(\alpha)$,

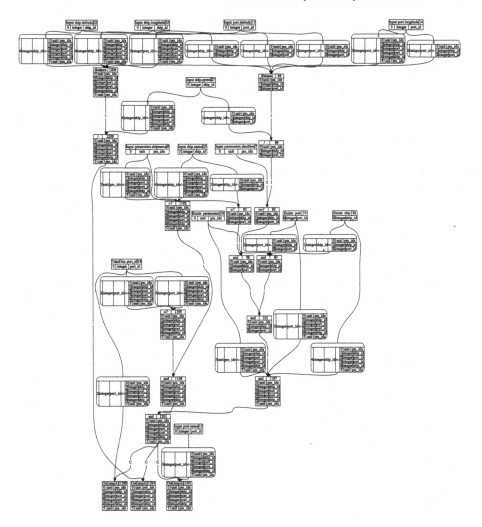

Fig. 5. Initial SDG

$\mathsf{t}(\beta \circ \alpha) = \mathsf{t}(\beta)$ and $\overline{\delta}(\beta \circ \alpha) = \overline{\delta}(\alpha) \circ \overline{\delta}(\beta)$, assuming that $\delta(v)$ is the identity mapping (which is always the case in the SDGs that we construct). After all arcs leaving v have been replaced, v is dead and can be removed by the previous simplification.

Splitting nodes with sum dimensions. A node v with $\mathsf{dim}(v) = \sum_{i=1}^{n} \prod_{j=1}^{m_i} X_{ij}$, where $n > 1$, is replaced with n nodes having the same operation, each corresponding to one component of $\mathsf{dim}(v)$. This transformation makes subsequent structural simplifications easier to apply.

Folding the "&"-nodes. If v and v' are both computing boolean conjunctions, and there is an arc α from v' to v, then we add arcs from all predecessors of v' to v (with the correct $\overline{\delta}(\cdot)$-mapping) and remove the arc α. If there were no other arcs leaving v', then it is dead.

Joining nodes with identical computation. If two nodes have the same operation and the same inputs, they can be turned to a single node. In our SDGs, the recognition of these nodes is complicated by the need to determine if a suitable isomorphism between their dimensions exists.

Reducing the dimension of a node. In our SDG-s, the dimensions of nodes are products of elements of $\mathcal{S}$. If for some node v in SDG, the predecessors of the nodes corresponding to v in the infinite dependency graph do not depend on some component of the elements in $\dim(v)$, then this component may be removed from $\dim(v)$.

Joining components of dimensions. Let v be a node that computes a boolean result, and let $\dim(v) = \prod_{i=1}^{n} X_i$. Suppose that we have deduced that there are indices $i, j \in \{1, \ldots, n\}$, such that a node $(v, (x_1, \ldots, x_n))$ in the expanded dependency graph may be true only if $x_i = x_j$. This may happen in a work-flow that creates complex joins of tables, joining the same table many times while requiring the primary keys to be equal; we use these equality checks to deduce that v implies $x_i = x_j$. It may also happen due to uniqueness constraints on attributes, when conjunctions of several comparisons involving these attributes are formed. If we have identified that the i-th and the j-th component of $\dim(v)$ have to be equal for v to be true, and when v being false only implies that certain outputs are not made, then we can identify these components and thereby reduce the dimension of v. This reduction works differently from the previous simplification, and has to be propagated along the SDG in both directions.

Arithmetic simplifications. A conjunction with a single input, or a sum with a single input can be turned to an ID node. A conjunction with a FALSE-input can be turned to FALSE-node (with no inputs). A COALESCE-operation can also be simplified if we know that some of its arguments certainly are, or certainly are not NULL.

Figure 6 depicts the results of the simplifications applied to the SDG in Fig. 5.

4.2   Presenting the Result of the Analysis

The dependencies and conditions are depicted in our final, simplified SDG, but they are not given in terms of certain rows existing or not existing in the tables of the database. To present the outcome, we have to map from the product of elements of $\mathcal{S}$ back into tables. Let $v_\bullet$ be a particular output node, for which we are interested in the computation of the value it outputs, as well as in the condition that must be satisfied for the output to take place. We perform the following steps for obtaining the description of the outputs from $v_\bullet$.

– First, we remove all output nodes except $v_\bullet$ from the SDG, and remove all dead nodes from it. After that, we will transform the directed acyclic SDG into a tree T, by duplicating nodes with several outgoing arcs. The root of T is $v_\bullet$. The leaves of T are the input nodes, referring to a particular attribute in a particular table.

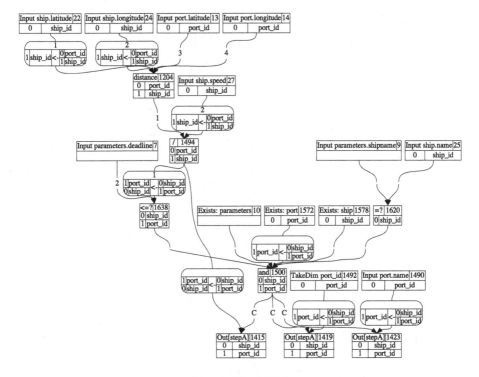

Fig. 6. Final SDG

- Let $\mathcal{PC}$ be the set of all *dimension components* (i.e. the elements of $\mathcal{S}$) of all nodes in T, formally

$$\mathcal{PC} = \bigcup_{v \in V(T)} \left(\{(v, i, X_i) \mid \dim(v) = \prod_{i=1}^{n} X_i\} \cup \{(v, -i, X_i) \mid \overrightarrow{\dim}(v) = \prod_{i=1}^{n} X_i\} \right).$$

Let $\mathcal{C}$ be the set $\mathcal{PC}$ factored by an equivalence relation generated by the $\delta(\cdot)$-mappings of all vertices and the $\overline{\delta}(\cdot)$-mappings of all arcs in T. The set $\mathcal{C}$ is the inventory of all *different* dimension components that occur in T.

- Each input node refers to a table, and its dimension refers to some elements of $\mathcal{C}$. The inputs nodes with the same table and the same elements of $\mathcal{C}$ correspond to the same row of the table. We replace the input nodes, and forget the dimensions and their maps of the internal nodes and arcs. For input nodes with partially overlapping sets of elements of $\mathcal{C}$, we introduce the equality checks of the respective components of the table rows, which must be satisfied for the node $v_\bullet$ to output anything.

The result, when $v_\bullet$ is the node with ID 1415 in Fig. 6, is depicted in Fig. 7.

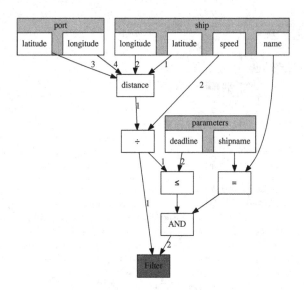

Fig. 7. Representation of the computations

5   Related Work

One of the most prominent examples of methods to quantify the potential disclosure of information is that of differential privacy, which has been widely studied
in the context of program analysis, using e.g. types [5] or theorem proving [2].
These techniques allow one to reason about the theoretical bounds of the amount
information revealed by a program on its output relative to its input. In a similar vein, techniques have been proposed to analyze sensitivity and differential
privacy for database queries expressed in SQL [6], and other SQL-like languages
(e.g. PINQ) [7]. Here, the reasoning on sensitivity is formulated in terms of individual database queries and the effects on the output of those queries with respect
to variations on the input tables. In recent work [4,10], we have extended the
results on differential privacy to reason about not only one single computation
step, but to assess the overall differential privacy of a data processing workflows,
which require the aggregation of the sensitivity of the steps in a workflow that
can be observed by one stakeholder. The goal of works on differential privacy is
the to derive theoretical bounds of the amount of information that a stakeholder
can infer from the outputs of programs or steps on a workflow. Conversely, in
this work we look not at quantifying the disclosure of information but rather
providing an insight on what is disclosed and on the conditions that must hold
for that disclosure to happen.

Also close to our setting is the work on information leak detection on business
process models reported in [1]. Such method takes as input workflows on which
tasks have been classified in levels of confidentiality, which can be either high
or low. By using a reachability analysis, the method is capable of identifying
structures on the workflow (e.g. sequencing of tasks, mutual exclusion, etc) where

information may be leaked to stakeholders, when changes between domains of confidentiality are not properly guarded. In contrast, our method considers the underlying computation (e.g. SQL code) and identifies what information as well as the conditions that will be revealed after having executing a SQL workflow.

6 Conclusions and Future Work

The paper presented an analysis technique to determine what information from each input table is disclosed by each output table of a SQL Workflow, and under what conditions this disclosure occurs. The proposed technique has been implemented on top of the Pleak open-source business process privacy analysis toolset. The source code of the toolset is available at https://github.com/pleak-tools while a demonstrator is available at http://pleak.io/.

The current technique operates over unprotected workflows, meaning workflows that do not make use of any Privacy-Enhancing Technologies (PETs) such as multi-party computation, encryption, or differential privacy. In future work, we plan to extend the technique to take as input workflows where some of the tasks have PETs attached to them. This extension would allow analysts to perform "what-if" privacy analysis. Concretely, an analyst would be able to see how the addition, removal, or modification of a PET in a workflow affects the information that is disclosed to different parties.

Another extension is the ability to compare a disclosure report against a privacy policy. This capability would allow an analyst to determine what additional PETs could be added to a given process in order to fulfill a privacy policy.

Acknowledgments. This research was funded by the Air Force Research laboratory (AFRL) and Defense Advanced Research Projects Agency (DARPA) under contract FA8750-16-C-0011. The views expressed are those of the author(s) and do not reflect the official policy or position of the Department of Defense or the U.S. Government.

A Translating SQL Workflows to Internal Representation

The translation of a query Q to a summary dependency graph (SDG) proceeds by first translating the database schema, then performing the syntax-directed translation of the actual query Q, followed by the addition of output nodes. We call the intermediate graphs *Partial Summary Dependency Graphs* (PDSG), where the partiality indicates the lack of output nodes.

Let G be a PSDG and consider a relation schema r with attributes $a_1, \ldots, a_n$. A *representation of r in G* is a mapping $R : \{\exists, a_1, \ldots, a_n\} \to V(G)$, such that $\dim(R(\exists)) = \dim(R(a_1)) = \cdots = \dim(R(a_n))$, the output type of each $R(a_i)$ matches with the type of a_i, and the output type of $R(\exists)$ is boolean. We write $\dim(R)$ for $\dim(R(\exists))$. A *representation* of a database schema *dbs in G* is a mapping from the contained relations into their representations in G.

Translating a Database Schema. The translation of a database schema *dbs* returns a PSDG G_{dbs}, as well as a representation R_{dbs} of *dbs* in it. These are the following:

- Let $t : r$ be a table declaration in *dbs*, where r is the relation schema $r(a_1 : D_1, \ldots, a_n : D_n; \text{index}_r)$, with certain attributes belonging to the index. W.l.o.g. let $a_1, \ldots, a_h$ be the index attributes. The graph G will contain nodes $v_{\exists}^t$ and v_i^t for $1 \leq i \leq n$. The input dimension and the dimension of all nodes is $\mathcal{I} = \prod_{i=1}^h D_i$. All nodes are input nodes. During the execution, the instance $(x_1, \ldots, x_h)$ of the node v_i^t is supposed to carry the value of the attribute a_i in the row of the table t that corresponds to the index value $(a_1 = x_1, \ldots, a_h = x_h)$. The instance $(x_1, \ldots, x_h)$ of the node $v_{\exists}^t$ carries the value true iff the table t has a row with index value $(a_1 = x_1, \ldots, a_h = x_h)$.
- The representation R_{dbs} maps each table t to the mapping $\{\exists \mapsto v_{\exists}^t\} \cup \{a_i \mapsto v_i^t \mid 1 \leq i \leq |t|\}$.

Translating the Query. The translation $\mathcal{G}$ of a query Q against a database with schema *dbs* takes as input a PSDG $G_\circ$ and a representation R_{dbs} of *dbs* in it. It returns a new PSDG $G_\bullet$ (which is obtained from $G_\circ$ by adding zero or more nodes to it) and a representation of $\mathbf{attr}(Q)$ in $G_\bullet$, where $\mathbf{attr}(Q)$ is the schema of the output relation of Q.

The translation $\mathcal{G}$ may call the translation $\mathcal{E}$ for expressions e. It takes as input a PSDG $G_\circ$ and a representation R of a relation schema in $G_\circ$. This relation schema must contain all attributes used by e. The translation $\mathcal{E}$ returns a new PSDG $G_\bullet$ and a node $v_e \in V(G_\bullet)$. The translation $\mathcal{E}$ works as follows.

- $\mathcal{E}[\![a]\!](G_\circ, R)$ returns $G_\circ$ and $R(a)$.
- $\mathcal{E}[\![\otimes(e_1, \ldots, e_k)]\!](G_\circ, R)$ calls $\mathcal{E}[\![e_1]\!], \ldots, \mathcal{E}[\![e_k]\!]$ one after another. Let the output of $\mathcal{E}[\![e_i]\!]$ be G_i and v_i. Then the inputs to $\mathcal{E}[\![e_i]\!]$ are G_{i-1} (with $G_0 \equiv G_\circ$) and R. After obtaining G_k, add a new node v to the graph. Its label is $\otimes$, and its dimension and input dimension are both $\dim(R)$. Also add arcs $\alpha_1, \ldots, \alpha_k$ to the graph, going from nodes $v_1, \ldots, v_k$ to the node v. For all i, the mapping $\bar{\delta}(\alpha_i)$ is equal to the identity map on $\dim(R)$. Return the modified graph G_k and the vertex v.

The translation $\mathcal{G}$ works as follows.

- $\mathcal{G}[\![t]\!](G_\circ, R_{dbs})$ returns $G_\circ$ and $R_{dbs}(t)$.
- $\mathcal{G}[\![Q_1 \times \cdots \times Q_k]\!](G_\circ, R_{dbs})$ calls $\mathcal{G}[\![Q_1]\!], \ldots, \mathcal{G}[\![Q_k]\!]$ one after another. Let the output of $\mathcal{G}[\![Q_i]\!]$ be G_i and R_i^Q. Then the inputs to $\mathcal{G}[\![Q_i]\!]$ are G_{i-1} (with $G_0 \equiv G_\circ$) and R_{dbs}. After obtaining G_k and $R_1^Q, \ldots, R_k^Q$, we add the following nodes and arcs to G_k:
  - Let $\mathcal{I} = \prod_{i=1}^k \dim(R_i^Q)$.
  - Add a node $v_\exists$. The label of this node is "&" (boolean conjunction). Its dimension and input dimension are both $\mathcal{I}$.
  - For each $i \in \{1, \ldots, k\}$ add an arc $\alpha_{\exists,i}$ from the node $R_i^Q(\exists)$ to $v_\exists$. The mapping $\bar{\delta}(\alpha_{\exists,i})$ is the canonical projection from $\mathcal{I}$ to its i-th component $\dim(R_i^Q)$.

- For each $i \in \{1, \ldots, k\}$ and each attribute $a_j \in \mathbf{attr}(Q_i)$ add a node $v_{i,j}$. The label of this node is "ID" (the identity mapping). Its dimension and input dimension are both $\mathcal{I}$.
- Also, add an arc $\alpha_{i,j}$ from $R_i^Q(a_j)$ to $v_{i,j}$. The mapping $\overline{\delta}(\alpha_{i,j})$ is the canonical projection from $\mathcal{I}$ to its i-th component $\mathsf{dim}(R_i^Q)$.

Let the output PSDG $G_\bullet$ be the modified graph G_k. The output representation R maps $\exists$ to $v_\exists$ and the attribute a_j in $\mathbf{attr}(Q_i)$ to $v_{i,j}$.

- $\mathcal{G}[\![[Q]\!]_{a \to a'}]\!](G_\circ, R_{dbs})$ runs $(G_\bullet, R) = \mathcal{G}[\![Q]\!](G_\circ, R_{dbs})$. It returns $G_\bullet$ and $R[a' \mapsto R(a)]$.
- $\mathcal{G}[\![\sigma(Q; e)]\!](G_\circ, R_{dbs})$ runs $(G', R) = \mathcal{G}[\![Q]\!](G_\circ, R_{dbs})$ and $(G'', v_?) = \mathcal{E}[\![e]\!](G', R)$. It adds a node $v_\exists$ to G''. The label of this node is "&" and both its dimension and input dimension are $\mathsf{dim}(R)$. The node $v_\exists$ has two inputs, from $R(\exists)$ and from $v_?$. The $\overline{\delta}(\cdot)$-mappings of both respective arcs are the identity mappings over $\mathsf{dim}(R)$. Let $G_\bullet$ be the modified graph G''. The translation returns $G_\bullet$ and $R[\exists \mapsto v_\exists]$.
- $\mathcal{G}[\![\pi_{a_1,\ldots,a_k}(Q)]\!](G_\circ, R_{dbs})$ runs $(G_\bullet, R) = \mathcal{G}[\![Q]\!](G_\circ, R_{dbs})$. It returns $G_\bullet$ and R restricted to $\{\exists, a_1, \ldots, a_k\}$.
- $\mathcal{G}[\![\mathsf{col}_{a \leftarrow e}(Q)]\!](G_\circ, R_{dbs})$ runs $(G', R) = \mathcal{G}[\![Q]\!](G_\circ, R_{dbs})$ and $(G_\bullet, v_e) = \mathcal{E}[\![e]\!](G', R)$. It returns $G_\bullet$ and $R[a \mapsto v_e]$.
- $\mathcal{G}[\![\mathsf{let}\ t = Q_1\ \mathsf{in}\ Q_2]\!](G_\circ, R_{dbs})$ runs $(G', R_0) = \mathcal{G}[\![Q_1]\!](G_\circ, R_{dbs})$, followed by $(G_\bullet, R) = \mathcal{G}[\![Q_2]\!](G', R_{dbs}[t \mapsto R_0])$. It returns $G_\bullet$ and R.
- $\mathcal{G}[\![Q_1 \cup Q_2]\!](G_\circ, R_{dbs})$ runs

$$(G', R') = \mathcal{G}[\![Q_1]\!](G_\circ, R_{dbs})$$
$$(G'', R'') = \mathcal{G}[\![Q_2]\!](G', R_{dbs}).$$

For each attribute $a \in \mathbf{attr}(Q_1) = \mathbf{attr}(Q_2)$ it will then add a node v_a to G'', with the operation "ID" and its dimension and input dimension both being equal to $\mathsf{dim}(R') + \mathsf{dim}(R'')$. The mapping $\delta(v_a)$ is the identity mapping. The node v_a has a single incoming arc α_a, which has *two* sources— $R'(a)$ and $R''(a)$. The mapping $\overline{\delta}(\alpha_a)$ is the identity mapping from $\overrightarrow{\mathsf{dim}}(v_a)$ to $\mathsf{dim}(R'(a)) + \mathsf{dim}(R''(a))$.

We also add a node $v_\exists$ to the graph G'' with the same dimension, input dimension and $\delta(\cdot)$-mapping as described in the previous paragraph. The operation in this node is again "ID" (boolean disjunction), and it again has a single incoming arc $\alpha_\exists$ with two sources: $R'(\exists)$ and $R''(\exists)$, with the mapping $\overline{\delta}(()\alpha_\exists)$ again being the identity map.

Let the output PDSG $G_\bullet$ be the graph G'' with the added nodes and arcs. The output representation R maps $\exists$ to $v_\exists$ and each attribute a to v_a.

- $\mathcal{G}[\![Q_1 \cap Q_2]\!](G_\circ, R_{dbs})$ runs

$$(G', R') = \mathcal{G}[\![\sigma(Q_1 \times [Q_2]_{a:\mathbf{attr}(Q_2) \to a'};\ \bigwedge_{a \in \mathbf{attr}(Q_1)} a = a')]\!](G_\circ, R_{dbs})$$

first, while also keeping the representation R_1 that was produced while $\mathcal{G}[\![Q_1]\!](G_\circ, R_{dbs})$ was run as a subroutine. Here the write-up $[Q_2]_{a:\mathbf{attr}(Q_2) \to a'}$

denotes that we have renamed all attributes a of Q_2 into their primed versions.

We add to G' a node $v_\exists$ with the operation "$\bigvee$" (boolean disjunction). We let $\dim(v_\exists) = \dim(R_1)$ and $\overrightarrow{\dim}(v_\exists) = \dim(R')$. Recall that $\dim(R')$ is equal to the Cartesian product of $\dim(R_1)$ and the dimension of the nodes resulting from the translation of the query Q_2. The mapping $\delta(v_\exists)$ is the natural projection to the first component of this product.

As $\dim(v_\exists) \neq \overrightarrow{\dim}(v_\exists)$, this node may have a single incoming arc. This arc comes from the node $R'(\exists)$, its $\overline{\delta}(\cdot)$-mapping is the identity mapping.

We return the graph G' with the extra node and arc. As the output representation, we return $R_1[\exists \mapsto v_\exists]$.

- $\mathcal{G}[\![Q_1 \ltimes_e Q_2]\!](G_\circ, R_{dbs})$ runs

$$(G', R_2) = \mathcal{G}[\![Q_1 \times Q_2]\!](G_\circ, R_{dbs})$$
$$(G'', v_e) = \mathcal{E}[\![e]\!](G', R_2).$$

We also keep the representation R_1 that was produced when $\mathcal{G}[\![Q_1]\!](G_\circ, R_{dbs})$ was run as a subroutine. After that, we add the following nodes and arcs to G''.

- Node v_1, operation "&", with dimension and input dimension equal to $\dim(R_2)$. Its inputs are v_e and $R_2(\exists)$.
- Node v_2, operation "$\bigvee$". Its dimension is equal to $\dim(R_1)$ and its input dimension to $\dim(R_2)$. The mapping $\delta(v_2)$ is the natural projection from the second to the first. The input to v_2 is the node v_1.
- Node v_3, operation "NOT". Its dimension and input dimension are equal to $\dim(R_1)$. Its input is the node v_2.
- Node v_4, operation "&". Its inputs are v_3 and $R_1(\exists)$.

For all arcs described above, their $\overline{\delta}(\cdot)$-mapping is the identity mapping. The translation returns the PSDG G'' together with added nodes and arcs. As the output representation, it returns $R_1[\exists \mapsto v_4]$.

- $\mathcal{G}[\![\text{group}_{(a'_1 \otimes_1), \ldots, (a'_l, \otimes_l)}^{a_1, \ldots, a_k}(Q)]\!](G_\circ, R_{dbs})$ first runs $(G', R') = \mathcal{G}[\![Q]\!](G_\circ, R_{dbs})$. It will determine the types $D_1, \ldots, D_k$ of the attributes $a_1, \ldots, a_k$ of Q. These types must be elements of $\mathcal{S}$. The following nodes and arcs are then added to G':

- Nodes $v_1^{TD}, \ldots, v_k^{TD}$. These are input nodes of the SDG. The dimension of v_i^{TD} is D_i. In the infinite dependency graph, a node v corresponding to the value $x \in D_i$ and the node v_i^{TD}, is expected to carry the value x. Let $\mathcal{I} = D_1 \times \cdots \times D_k$.
- Nodes $v_1^=, \ldots, v_k^=$. The operation of these nodes is "=" (equality check). The dimension and input dimension of these nodes is $\dim(R') \times \mathcal{I}$. The node $v_i^=$ has two inputs: v_i^{TD} and $R'(a_i)$. The $\overline{\delta}(\cdot)$-mappings for the arcs connecting these nodes are the natural projections.
- Node $v^=$. The operation of this node is "&". Its dimension and input dimension are both $\dim(R') \times \mathcal{I}$. Its inputs are the nodes $v_1^=, \ldots, v_k^=$.
- Node $v_\exists$. The operation of this node is "$\bigvee$". Its dimension is $\mathcal{I}$ and its input dimension is $\dim(R') \times \mathcal{I}$. The mapping $\delta(w_\exists)$ is the natural projection. Node $v_\exists$ receives its input from $v^=$.

- Nodes $v_1^f, \ldots, v_l^f$. The operation of these nodes is "Output"; this operation takes two arguments and returns the first one only if the second one is true. Their dimension and input dimension are $\dim(R') \times \mathcal{I}$. The inputs of the node v_j^f are $v^=$ (for the first, "conditioning" argument) and $R'(a_j')$ (for the second, "value" argument). The $\overline{\delta}(\cdot)$-mapping for the arc connecting to the first input is the identity mapping, while for the arc connecting to the second input is the natural projection from $\dim(R') \times \mathcal{I}$ to $\dim(R')$.

- Nodes $v_1^\otimes, \ldots, v_l^\otimes$. The operation of the node $v_j^\otimes$ is "$\bigotimes_j$". The dimension of $v_j^\otimes$ is $\mathcal{I}$, while its input dimension is $\dim(R') \times \mathcal{I}$. The mapping $\delta(v_j^\otimes)$ is the natural projection. The input to the node $v_j^\otimes$ is the node v_j^f.

We see that the expansions of the nodes $v_j^\otimes$ in the infinite dependency graph perform the actual aggregations of the values of the dataset resulting from the query Q. We have implicitly assumed that the NULL-values among the inputs of the operations $\bigotimes_j$ do not change their output value.

The translation returns the graph G' together with the added nodes and arcs. The output representation R is the following:

- $R(\exists) = w_\exists$;
- $R(a_i) = v_i^{\mathrm{TD}}$ for the attributes $a_1, \ldots, a_k$;
- $R(a_j') = v_j^\otimes$ for the attributes $a_1', \ldots, a_l'$.

Adding Output Nodes. Let the query Q be translated by calling $\mathcal{G}[\![Q]\!]$ on the translation of the database schema. The result of $\mathcal{G}[\![Q]\!]$ is a PSDG G and a representation R of $\mathbf{attr}(Q)$ in G. We add the following nodes and arcs to G:

– For each $a_i \in \mathbf{attr}(Q)$, add nodes v_i and v_i^O. For both of them, their dimension and input dimension are equal to $\dim(R)$. Node v_i is an internal node, while v_i^O is an output node. There is an arc from v_i to v_i^O; its $\overline{\delta}(\cdot)$-mapping is the identity mapping on $\dim(R)$. There are two arcs into v_i, first from $R(\exists)$ and second from $R(a_i)$. Their $\overline{\delta}(\cdot)$-mappings are also the identity mappings on $\dim(R)$. The operation of v_i is named "Output". The semantics of an "Output" operation is to return the second argument, if the first argument is true, and to return NULL otherwise.

References

1. Accorsi, R., Lehmann, A., Lohmann, N.: Information leak detection in business process models: theory, application, and tool support. Inf. Syst. **47**, 244–257 (2015)
2. Barthe, G., Köpf, B., Olmedo, F., Béguelin, S.Z.: Probabilistic relational reasoning for differential privacy. ACM Trans. Program. Lang. Syst. **35**(3), 9 (2013)
3. Colesky, M., Hoepman, J.-H., Hillen, C.: A critical analysis of privacy design strategies. In: IEEE Security and Privacy Workshops (SP), pp. 33–40. IEEE Computer Society (2016)
4. Dumas, M., García-Bañuelos, L., Laud, P.: Differential privacy analysis of data processing workflows. In: Kordy, B., Ekstedt, M., Kim, D.S. (eds.) GraMSec 2016. LNCS, vol. 9987, pp. 62–79. Springer, Cham (2016). https://doi.org/10.1007/978-3-319-46263-9_4

5. Gaboardi, M., Haeberlen, A., Hsu, J., Narayan, A., Pierce, B.C.: Linear dependent types for differential privacy. In: Proceedings of POPL 2013, pp. 357–370. ACM (2013)
6. Johnson, N., Near, J.P., Song, D.: Towards practical differential privacy for SQL queries. Proc. VLDB Endow. **11**(5), 526–539 (2018)
7. McSherry, F.: Privacy integrated queries: an extensible platform for privacy-preserving data analysis. In: Proceedings of SIGMOD 2009, pp. 19–30. ACM (2009)
8. OMG: Business Process Model and Notation (BPMN), Version 2.0. Technical report, Object Management Group, January 2011
9. Perumal, S., Mahanti, A.: A graph-search based algorithm for verifying workflow graphs. In: Proceedings of DEXA 2005, pp. 992–996. IEEE Computer Society (2005)
10. Pettai, M., Laud, P.: Combining differential privacy and mutual information for analyzing leakages in workflows. In: Maffei, M., Ryan, M. (eds.) POST 2017. LNCS, vol. 10204, pp. 298–319. Springer, Heidelberg (2017). https://doi.org/10.1007/978-3-662-54455-6_14
11. Tšahhirov, I., Laud, P.: Application of dependency graphs to security protocol analysis. In: Barthe, G., Fournet, C. (eds.) TGC 2007. LNCS, vol. 4912, pp. 294–311. Springer, Heidelberg (2008). https://doi.org/10.1007/978-3-540-78663-4_20

On Linear Logic, Functional
Programming, and Attack Trees

Harley Eades III[1](✉), Jiaming Jiang[2], and Aubrey Bryant[1]

[1] Computer Science, Augusta University, Augusta, USA
harley.eades@gmail.com
[2] Computer Science, North Carolina State University, Raleigh, USA

Abstract. This paper has two main contributions. The first is a new linear logical semantics of causal attack trees in four-valued truth tables. Our semantics is very simple and expressive, supporting specializations, and supports the *ideal* semantics of causal attack trees, and partially supporting the *filter* semantics of causal attack trees. Our second contribution is Lina, a new embedded, in Haskell, domain specific functional programming language for conducting threat analysis using attack trees. Lina has many benefits over existing tools; for example, Lina allows one to specify attack trees very abstractly, which provides the ability to develop libraries of attack trees, furthermore, Lina is compositional, allowing one to break down complex attack trees into smaller ones that can be reasoned about and analyzed incrementally. Furthermore, Lina supports automatically proving properties of attack trees, such as equivalences and specializations, using Maude and the semantics introduced in this paper.

1   Introduction

Attack trees are perhaps the most popular graphical model used to conduct threat analysis of both physical and virtual secure systems. They were made popular by Bruce Schneier in the late nineties [16]. In those early years attack trees were studied and used as a syntactic tool to help guide analysis. However, as systems grew more complex the need for a semantics of attack trees become apparent; after all, without a proper semantics how can we safely manipulate attack trees, extend their expressivity, or compare them?

A number of different models of attack trees have been proposed: a model in Boolean algebras [10,11,15], series-parallel pomsets [12], Petri nets [13], and tree automata [1]. There have also been various extensions, such as, adding sequential composition [6], and defense nodes [9,10]. All of these models and extensions have their benefits, but at the heart of them all is logic.

The model in Boolean algebras was the first and most elegant model of attack trees, but it failed to capture the process aspect of attack trees, that is, the fact that base attacks are actual processes that need to be carried out, and the branching nodes compose these processes in different ways. Thus, the

© Springer Nature Switzerland AG 2019
G. Cybenko et al. (Eds.): GraMSec 2018, LNCS 11086, pp. 71–89, 2019.
https://doi.org/10.1007/978-3-030-15465-3_5

community moved towards models of resources like parallel-series pomsets, Petri nets, and automata. However, the complexity of these models increased, and hence, comparing these models becomes difficult. Furthermore, this increased complexity makes it hard to decide which to use and under which circumstances. This difficulty can be resolved by recovering the elegant logical model of attack trees.

Linear Logic. It is fitting that attack trees are the most popular model used in threat analysis, because *linear logic*, one of the most widely studied logics used to reason about resources, is also an excellent candidate for modeling attack trees. In fact, Horne et al. [5] has already produced a number of interesting results. Most importantly, they show that attack trees can be modeled as formulas in linear logic, which then one can prove properties between attack trees by proving implications between them. Furthermore, by studying attack trees from a linear logical perspective they introduce a new property between attack trees called *specializations*. Prior to their paper the literature was primarily concerned with equality between attack trees, but the logical semantics of attack trees reveal how one can break these equalities up into directional rewrite rules. An attack tree is a *specialization* of another if the former is related to the later via these rewrite rules. The logical semantics model the rewrite rules as implications.

This paper has two main contributions. The first is a new simple linear logical semantics of causal attack trees – attack trees with sequential composition – in four-valued truth tables. It comes in two flavors: the ideal quaternary logic (Sect. 3.1) and the filterish quaternary logic (Sect. 3.2). These two types of semantics correspond to truth table semantics for Horne et al.'s [5] *ideal* and *filter* semantics of causal attack trees.

Functional Programming. Our second contribution is Lina, a new domain specific functional programming language for conducting threat analysis using attack trees. Consider the example attack trees in Fig. 1. Both of these contain actual Lina programs for each of the corresponding attack trees; in fact, every example in this paper is a Lina program. Lina supports causal attack trees with attributes or without; thus, there are two types of base attacks: base attacks with attributes, denoted `base_wa`, and base attacks with no attributes, denoted `base_na`; an example usage of the former can be found in Fig. 3. Lina is designed to be extremely simple, and to reflect the typical pseudocode found throughout the literature. However, Lina is more than just a simple definitional language.

Lina is an embedded domain-specific programming language whose host language is the Haskell programming language [7]. So, why Haskell? As security researchers and professionals, we are in the business of verifying the correctness of various systems. Thus, we should be taking advantage of verification tools to insure that our constructions, tools, and analysis are correct. By embedding Lina into Haskell, we are able to take advantage of cutting-edge verification tools while conducting threat analysis. For example, right out the box Lina supports property-based randomized testing using QuickCheck [2], and refinement types in Liquid Haskell [17] to verify properties of our attack trees or the attribute domains used while analyzing attack trees. Furthermore, Haskell's advanced type

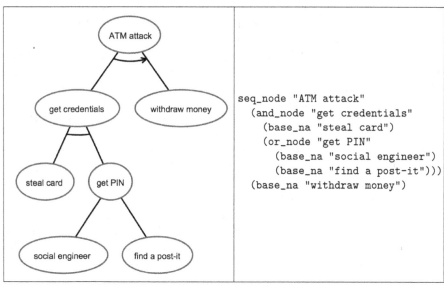

```
seq_node "ATM attack"
  (and_node "get credentials"
    (base_na "steal card")
    (or_node "get PIN"
      (base_na "social engineer")
      (base_na "find a post-it")))
  (base_na "withdraw money")
```

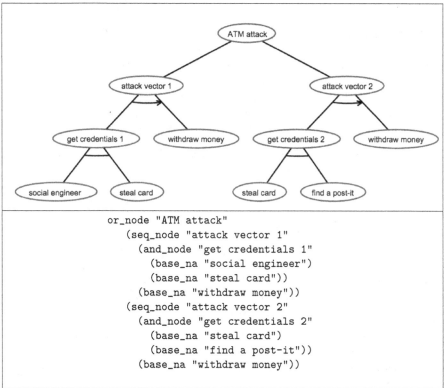

```
or_node "ATM attack"
  (seq_node "attack vector 1"
    (and_node "get credentials 1"
      (base_na "social engineer")
      (base_na "steal card"))
    (base_na "withdraw money"))
  (seq_node "attack vector 2"
    (and_node "get credentials 2"
      (base_na "steal card")
      (base_na "find a post-it"))
    (base_na "withdraw money"))
```

Fig. 1. Attack trees for an ATM attack from Figs. 1 and 2 of Kordy et al. [8] and their corresponding Lina scripts.

system helps catch bugs while we develop our attack trees and their attribute domains as a side-effect of type checking. Finally, functional programs are short, but not obfuscated, and hence allow for very compact and trustworthy programs.

That being said, we are designing Lina so that it can be used with very little Haskell experience. It is our hope that one will be able to make use of Lina without knowing Haskell, and we plan to develop new tooling to support this.

Lina approaches threat analysis from a programming language perspective, leading to a number of new advances. First, as Gadyatskaya and Trujillo-Rasua [4] argue, as a community we need to start building more automated means of conducting threat analysis, and there is no better way to build or connect automated tools than a programming language. Lina is perfect as a target for new tools, and it can be connected to existing tools fairly easily. In fact, Lina already supports automation using the automatic rewrite system Maude [3]; for example, the two attack trees in Fig. 1 can be automatically proven equivalent to each other in Lina. This is similar to Kordy's [8] SPTool, but Lina goes further and supports more than one backend rewrite system; for example, Lina is the first tool to support automatically proving specializations of attack trees. The user can choose which backend they wish to use.

2   Causal Attack Trees

We begin by introducing causal attack trees. This formulation of attack trees was first proposed by Jhawar et al. [6], where they called them SAND attack trees, however sequential composition does not always maintain the same properties as conjunction; for example, classically it is a self dual operator. Thus, we follow Horne et al.'s lead [5] and call them causal attack trees.

Definition 1. *Suppose $\mathbb{B}$ is a set of base attacks whose elements are denoted by b. Then an **attack tree** is defined by the following grammar:*

$$A, B, C, T := b \mid \mathsf{OR}(A, B) \mid \mathsf{AND}(A, B) \mid \mathsf{SEQ}(A, B)$$

Equivalence of attack trees, denoted by $A \approx B$, is defined as follows:

$\mathsf{OR}(A, A) \approx A$	$\mathsf{OR}(\mathsf{OR}(A, B), C) \approx \mathsf{OR}(A, \mathsf{OR}(B, C))$
$\mathsf{OR}(A, B) \approx \mathsf{OR}(B, A)$	$\mathsf{AND}(\mathsf{AND}(A, B), C) \approx \mathsf{AND}(A, \mathsf{AND}(B, C))$
$\mathsf{AND}(A, B) \approx \mathsf{AND}(B, A)$	$\mathsf{SEQ}(\mathsf{SEQ}(A, B), C) \approx \mathsf{SEQ}(A, \mathsf{SEQ}(B, C))$
	$\mathsf{AND}(A, \mathsf{OR}(B, C)) \approx \mathsf{OR}(\mathsf{AND}(A, B), \mathsf{AND}(A, C))$
	$\mathsf{SEQ}(A, \mathsf{OR}(B, C)) \approx \mathsf{OR}(\mathsf{SEQ}(A, B), \mathsf{SEQ}(A, C))$

Throughout the sequel we will show that the previous rules are sound with respect to our new model, but just as Horne et al. [5] did, we will then show that there are properties of attack trees that these rules do not support, but our semantics allows.

3   A Quaternary Semantics for Causal Attack Trees

Kordy et al. [10] gave a very elegant and simple semantics of attack-defense trees in Boolean algebras. Unfortunately, while their semantics is elegant, it does not capture the resource aspect of attack trees, it allows contraction, and it does not provide a means to model sequential composition. In this section we give a semantics of attack trees in the spirit of Kordy et al.'s using a four-valued logic. This section was formally verified in the Agda Proof Assistant [14][1].

We now give two types of quaternary semantics for casual attack trees. We do this by defining two four-valued logics we call quaternary logics. The propositional variables, elements of the set PVar, of our quaternary logics, denoted by P, Q, R, and S, range over the set $4 = \{0, \frac{1}{4}, \frac{1}{2}, 1\}$. We think of 0 and 1 as we usually do in Boolean algebras, but we think of $\frac{1}{4}$ and $\frac{1}{2}$ as intermediate values that can be used to break various structural rules[2]. In particular we will use these values to prevent exchange for sequential composition from holding, and contraction from holding for parallel and sequential composition.

We use the usual notion of equivalence between propositions; that is, propositions ϕ and ψ are considered equivalent, denoted by $\phi \equiv \psi$, if and only if they have the same truth tables. In addition, we define a notion of entailment for the quaternary logics. Denote by $P \leq_4 Q$ the usual natural number ordering restricted to 4. Then we have the following result immediately.

Lemma 1 (Entailment in the Quaternary Logics). $P \equiv Q$ *if and only if* $P \leq_4 Q$ *and* $Q \leq_4 P$

This result shows that we can break up the equivalence of attack trees into directional properties captured here by entailments, and hence, every equivalence proved throughout this section can also be used directionally.

3.1   The Ideal Quaternary Logic

The ideal semantics for casual attack trees was first proposed by Horne et al. [5]. In this section we give a simple truth table semantics that corresponds to their ideal semantics within the ideal quaternary logic.

Definition 2. *The logical connectives of the* ideal quaternary logic *are defined as follows:*

---

[1] The formalization can be found at https://github.com/MonoidalAttackTrees/ATLL-Formalization.

[2] Choosing $\frac{1}{4}$ and $\frac{1}{2}$ as the symbols for the intermediate values was arbitrary, and one can choose any symbols at all for these two values and the semantics will still be correct.

Parallel Composition:

$P \odot_I Q = 1$,
  where neither P nor Q are 0
$P \odot_I Q = 0$, otherwise

Sequential Composition:

$P \rhd_I Q = \frac{1}{2}$,
  where $P \in \{\frac{1}{2}, 1\}$ and $Q \neq 0$
$P \rhd_I Q = \frac{1}{4}$,
  where $P = \frac{1}{4}$ and $Q \neq 0$
$P \rhd_I Q = 0$, otherwise

Choice:

$P \sqcup_I Q = \max(P, Q)$

These definitions are carefully crafted to satisfy the necessary properties to model attack trees on the ideal semantics. Comparing these definitions with Kordy et al.'s [10] work we can see that choice is defined similarly, but parallel composition is not a product – ordinary conjunction – but rather a linear tensor product. Sequential composition is not actually definable in a Boolean algebra, and hence makes use of the intermediate values to insure that neither exchange nor contraction hold.

In order to model attack trees, the previously defined logical connectives must satisfy the appropriate equivalences corresponding to the equations between attack trees. We break these properties up into the following lemmata.

Lemma 2 (Basic Properties for Choice). *The following properties hold:*

1. $(P \sqcup_I Q) \equiv (Q \sqcup_I P)$
2. $((P \sqcup_I Q) \sqcup_I R) \equiv (P \sqcup_I (Q \sqcup_I R))$
3. $P \leq_4 (P \sqcup_I Q)$
4. $Q \leq_4 (P \sqcup_I Q)$
5. *If $P \leq_4 R$ and $Q \leq_4 R$, then $(P \sqcup_I Q) \leq_4 R$*
6. *If $P \leq_4 R$ and $Q \leq_4 S$, then $(P \sqcup_I Q) \leq_4 (R \sqcup_I S)$*

Proof. Each of the properties hold by comparing truth tables.

The previous lemma shows that choice has the same properties as Boolean disjunction. Hence, it is possible to show using these rules that $P \sqcup_I P \equiv P$ which follows from properties three, four, and five.

Lemma 3 (Basic Properties for Parallel Composition). *The following properties hold:*

1. $(P \odot_I P) \not\equiv P$
2. $(P \odot_I Q) \equiv (Q \odot_I P)$
3. $((P \odot_I Q) \odot_I R) \equiv (P \odot_I (Q \odot_I R))$
4. $(P \odot_I (Q \sqcup_I R)) \equiv ((P \odot_I Q) \sqcup_I (P \odot_I R))$
5. *If $P \leq_4 R$ and $Q \leq_4 S$, then $(P \odot_I Q) \leq_4 (R \odot_I S)$*

Proof. We give the proof of property one. The other properties hold by comparing truth tables. Suppose $P = \frac{1}{2}$, then $P \odot_I P = \frac{1}{2} \odot_I \frac{1}{2} = 1$, but 1 is not $\frac{1}{2}$.

The previous lemma shows that sequential composition is a linear tensor product. In particular, the first property guarantees that sequential composition does not contract parallel copies of attack trees into a single attack tree.

Lemma 4 (Basic Properties for Sequential Composition). *The following properties hold:*

1. $(P \rhd_I P) \not\equiv P$
2. $(P \rhd_I Q) \not\equiv (Q \rhd_I P)$
3. $(P \rhd_I (Q \rhd_I R)) \equiv ((P \rhd_I Q) \rhd_I R)$
4. $(P \rhd_I (Q \sqcup_I R)) \equiv ((P \rhd_I Q) \sqcup_I (P \rhd_I R))$
5. *If* $P \leq_4 R$ *and* $Q \leq_4 S$, *then* $(P \rhd_I Q) \leq_4 (R \rhd_I S)$

Proof. We give proofs for properties one and two, but the others hold by comparing truth tables. As for property one, suppose $P = 1$, then $P \rhd_I P = 1 \rhd_I 1 = \frac{1}{2}$, but 1 is not $\frac{1}{2}$. Now for property two, suppose $P = 1$ and $Q = \frac{1}{4}$, then $P \rhd_I Q = 1 \rhd_I \frac{1}{4} = \frac{1}{2}$, but $Q \rhd_I P = \frac{1}{4} \rhd_I 1 = \frac{1}{4}$.

This lemma is similar to the previous. However, property two guarantees that sequential composition is not commutative.

Lemma 5 (The Ideal Properties). *The following properties hold:*

1. $((P \odot_I Q) \rhd_I (R \odot_I S)) \leq_4 ((P \rhd_I R) \odot_I (Q \rhd_I S))$
2. $((P \odot_I Q) \rhd_I R) \leq_4 (P \odot_I (Q \rhd_I R))$
3. $(P \rhd_I (Q \odot_I R)) \leq_4 (Q \odot_I (P \rhd_I R))$
4. $(P \rhd_I Q) \leq_4 (P \odot_I Q)$

Proof. Each property holds by comparing truth tables.

At this point it is quite easy to model attack trees as formulas. The following defines their interpretation.

Definition 3. *Suppose* $\mathbb{B}$ *is some set of base attacks, and* $\nu : \mathbb{B} \to$ PVar *is an assignment of base attacks to propositional variables. Then we define the interpretation of attack trees to propositions as follows:*

$$
\begin{array}{llll}
[\![b \in \mathbb{B}]\!] & = & \nu(b) & \qquad [\![\mathsf{SEQ}(A,B)]\!] & = & [\![A]\!] \rhd_I [\![B]\!] \\
[\![\mathsf{AND}(A,B)]\!] & = & [\![A]\!] \odot_I [\![B]\!] & \qquad [\![\mathsf{OR}(A,B)]\!] & = & [\![A]\!] \sqcup_I [\![B]\!]
\end{array}
$$

We can use this semantics to prove equivalences between attack trees.

Lemma 6 (Equivalence of Attack Trees in the Ideal Quaternary Semantics). *Suppose* $\mathbb{B}$ *is some set of base attacks, and* $\nu : \mathbb{B} \to$ PVar *is an assignment of base attacks to propositional variables. Then for any attack trees* A *and* B, *if* $A \approx B$, *then* $[\![A]\!] \equiv [\![B]\!]$.

Proof. This proof holds by induction on the form of $A \approx B$.

3.2   The Filterish Quaternary Logic

We now introduce the filterish semantics for casual attack trees. This is a restricted notion of the filter semantics of Horne et al. [5]. We were unable to find a quaternary semantics for the full filter semantics, because we obtained contractions when attempting to satisfy the corresponding specialization properties in the filter model. We are unsure if these contradictions arise due to the fact that the semantics proposed here is intuitionistic while Horne et al. [5] use classical logic, or if four values just are not enough, or if we just have not been able to find it.

In this section we do as we did in the previous and define a quaternary logic called the *filterish quaternary logic*.

Definition 4. *The logical connectives of the* filterish quaternary logic *are defined as follows:*

Parallel Composition:
$P \odot_F Q = \frac{1}{2}$,
   where neither P nor Q are 0
$P \odot_F Q = 0$, *otherwise*

Sequential Composition:
$P \rhd_F Q = 1$,
   where $P \in \{\frac{1}{2}, 1\}$ and $Q \neq 0$
$P \rhd_F Q = \frac{1}{4}$,
   where $P = \frac{1}{4}$ and $Q \neq 0$
$P \rhd_F Q = 0$, *otherwise*

Choice:
$P \sqcup_F Q = \max(P, Q)$

We have the same basic properties as the ideal quaternary logic. We omit proofs, because they are similar to the corresponding properties in the ideal semantics.

Lemma 7 (Basic Properties for Choice). *The following properties hold:*

1. $(P \sqcup_F Q) \equiv (Q \sqcup_F P)$
2. $((P \sqcup_F Q) \sqcup_F R) \equiv (P \sqcup_F (Q \sqcup_F R))$
3. $P \leq_4 (P \sqcup_F Q)$
4. $Q \leq_4 (P \sqcup_F Q)$
5. *If $P \leq_4 R$ and $Q \leq_4 R$, then $(P \sqcup_F Q) \leq_4 R$*
6. *If $P \leq_4 R$ and $Q \leq_4 S$, then $(P \sqcup_F Q) \leq_4 (R \sqcup_F S)$*

Lemma 8 (Basic Properties for Parallel Composition). *The following properties hold:*

1. $(P \odot_F P) \not\equiv P$
2. $(P \odot_F Q) \equiv (Q \odot_F P)$
3. $((P \odot_F Q) \odot_F R) \equiv (P \odot_F (Q \odot_F R))$
4. $(P \odot_F (Q \sqcup_F R)) \equiv ((P \odot_F Q) \sqcup_F (P \odot_F R))$
5. *If $P \leq_4 R$ and $Q \leq_4 S$, then $(P \odot_F Q) \leq_4 (R \odot_F S)$*

Lemma 9 (Basic Properties for Sequential Composition). *The following properties hold:*

1. $(P \rhd_F P) \not\equiv P$

2. $(P \triangleright_F Q) \not\equiv (Q \triangleright_F P)$
3. $(P \triangleright_F (Q \triangleright_F R)) \equiv ((P \triangleright_F Q) \triangleright_F R)$
4. $(P \triangleright_F (Q \sqcup_F R)) \equiv ((P \triangleright_F Q) \sqcup_F (P \triangleright_F R))$
5. If $P \leq_4 R$ and $Q \leq_4 S$, then $(P \triangleright_F Q) \leq_4 (R \triangleright_F S)$

We now give the filterish properties that correspond to a subset of the filter properties proposed by Horne et al. [5].

Lemma 10 (The Filterish Properties). *The following properties hold:*

1. $((P \triangleright_F R) \odot_F (Q \triangleright_F S)) \leq_4 ((P \odot_F Q) \triangleright_F (R \odot_F S))$
2. $(P \odot_F (Q \triangleright_F R)) \leq_4 ((P \odot_F Q) \triangleright_F R)$

The remaining filter properties proposed by Horne et al. [5] actually fail in both directions.

Lemma 11. *There exists an P, Q, and R that cause the following properties to not hold:*

1. $(P \triangleright_F (Q \odot_F R)) \leq_r (Q \odot_F (P \triangleright_F R))$
2. $(P \triangleright_F Q) \leq_4 (P \odot_F Q)$

Interestingly, if we change Definition 4 so that all the basic properties hold and Lemma 11 holds, then the inequalities in Lemma 10 degenerate to equalities. We were unable to find a definition of the logical connectives that make all of the properties in both of the previous lemmas hold.

Just as we did for the ideal quaternary semantics we can show that we can model attack trees as formulas. The following defines their interpretation.

Definition 5. *Suppose $\mathbb{B}$ is some set of base attacks, and $\nu : \mathbb{B} \to$ PVar is an assignment of base attacks to propositional variables. Then we define the interpretation of attack trees to propositions as follows:*

$$
\begin{array}{llll}
[\![b \in \mathbb{B}]\!] & = & \nu(b) & \qquad [\![\mathsf{SEQ}(A, B)]\!] & = & [\![A]\!] \triangleright_F [\![B]\!] \\
[\![\mathsf{AND}(A, B)]\!] & = & [\![A]\!] \odot_F [\![B]\!] & \qquad [\![\mathsf{OR}(A, B)]\!] & = & [\![A]\!] \sqcup_F [\![B]\!]
\end{array}
$$

We can use this semantics to prove equivalences between attack trees.

Lemma 12 (Equivalence of Attack Trees in the Ideal Quaternary Semantics). *Suppose $\mathbb{B}$ is some set of base attacks, and $\nu : \mathbb{B} \to$ PVar is an assignment of base attacks to propositional variables. Then for any attack trees A and B, if $A \approx B$, then $[\![A]\!] \equiv [\![B]\!]$.*

Proof. This proof holds by induction on the form of $A \approx B$.

3.3 An Example Specialization

The quaternary logics introduced in the previous section do indeed capture all of the equivalences of attack trees, but they also support proving specializations. Consider the example attack trees in Fig. 2. In the ideal semantics attack tree C is a sound specialization of attack tree A, and attack tree B is a sound specialization of attack tree A. Attack tree C requires the attacker to break into the system before they can steal the backup, but attack tree A does not require this. Then attack tree B has dropped bribing the sysadmin and simply requires the attacker to just steal the backups. Notice that none of the attack trees in Fig. 2 are equivalent. So how do we prove these specializations are sound? We prove that they are related through an entailment rather than an equivalence.

```
A.
 and_node "obtain secret"
  (or_node "obtain encrypted file"
   (base_na "bribe sysadmin")
   (base_na "steal backup"))
  (seq_node "obtain password"
   (base_na "break into system")
   (base_na "install keylogger"))
```

```
B.
 seq_node "break in, obtain secret"
  (base_na "break into system")
  (and_node "obtain secret inside"
   (base_na "install keylogger")
   (base_na "steal backup"))
```

```
C.
 or_node "obtain secret"
  (and_node "obtain secret via sysadmin"
   (base_na "bribe sysadmin")
   (seq_node "obtain password"
    (base_na "break into system")
    (base_na "install keylogger")))
  (seq_node "break in, obtain secret"
   (base_na "break into system")
   (and_node "obtain secret inside"
    (base_na "install keylogger")
    (base_na "steal backup")))
```

Fig. 2. Encrypted data attack from Figs. 1(A), 3(B) and 2(C) of Horne et al. [5].

Definition 6. *An attack tree A is a sound specialization of an attack B if and only if $[\![A]\!] \leq_4 [\![B]\!]$.*

We can now formally prove that the attack tree C is a specialization of attack tree A, and that attack tree B is a specialization of attack tree A from Fig. 2.

Example 1. First, consider the following assignment:

$$a := \text{"bribe sysadmin"} \qquad b := \text{"break into system"}$$
$$c := \text{"install keylogger"} \quad d := \text{"steal backup"}$$

Then we have the following interpretations:

$$[\![A]\!] = [\![\mathsf{AND}(\mathsf{OR}(a,d),\mathsf{SEQ}(b,c))]\!] \quad [\![B]\!] = [\![\mathsf{SEQ}(b,\mathsf{AND}(c,d))]\!]$$
$$= (a \sqcup_I d) \odot_I (b \rhd_I c) \qquad\qquad = b \rhd_I (c \odot_I d)$$

$$[\![C]\!] = [\![\mathsf{OR}(\mathsf{AND}(a,\mathsf{SEQ}(b,c)),\mathsf{SEQ}(b,\mathsf{AND}(c,d)))]\!]$$
$$= (a \odot_I (b \rhd_I c)) \sqcup_I (b \rhd_I (c \odot_I d))$$

We reuse the same names for base attacks across the interpretations above. Finally, we have the following two entailments:

$[\![C]\!] \leq_4 [\![A]\!]$:	$[\![B]\!] \leq_I [\![A]\!]$:
$(a \odot_I (b \rhd_I c)) \sqcup_I (b \rhd_I (c \odot_I d))$	$b \rhd_I (c \odot_I d)$
$\leq_4 (a \odot_I (b \rhd_I c)) \sqcup_I (b \rhd_I (d \odot_I c))$	$\leq_4 b \rhd_I (c \odot_I (a \sqcup_I d))$
$\leq_4 (a \odot_I (b \rhd_I c)) \sqcup_I (d \odot_I (b \rhd_I c))$	$\leq_4 b \rhd_I ((a \sqcup_I d) \odot_I c)$
$\leq_4 (a \sqcup_I d) \odot_I (b \rhd_I c)$	$\leq_4 (a \sqcup_I d) \odot_I (b \rhd_I c)$

Notice that neither $[\![A]\!] \leq_4 [\![C]\!]$ nor $[\![A]\!] \leq_4 [\![B]\!]$ hold, and thus, equivalences cannot prove the previous properties.

4 Lina: An EDSL for Conducting Threat Analysis Using Causal Attack Trees

All of the models mentioned in this paper have been incorporated into a new embedded domain specific language (EDSL) for conducting threat analysis called Lina[3] which means small, young palm tree, but we constructed the name by combining the words linear and attack.

Lina is embedded inside of Haskell, a statically-typed functional programming language. The most important property of any EDSL is that they subsume the entirety of their host language, and can be prototyped quite rapidly. Haskell contributes several advantages, such as cutting edge verification tools, and a strong type system for catching bugs quickly.

Lina currently supports three types of causal attack trees:

- Process Attack Trees: these are attack trees with no attributes at all,
- Attributed Process Attack Trees: these are attack trees with attributes on the base attacks only. This is an intermediate representation used to build full attack trees.
- Full Attack Trees: these are attributed process attack trees with an associated attribute domain.

Internally, we represent causal attack trees by a simple data type, called IAT, whose nodes are labeled with an integer identifier we call ID. We then define each type of attack tree as a record (labeled tuple):

---

[3] Lina is under active development and its implementation can be found online at https://github.com/MonoidalAttackTrees/Lina.

```
-- Attributed Process Attack Tree          -- Process Attack Tree
data APAttackTree attribute label =        type PAttackTree label = APAttackTree () label
   APAttackTree {
     process_tree :: IAT,                   -- Full Attack Tree
     labels :: B.Bimap label ID,            data AttackTree attribute label = AttackTree {
     attributes :: M.Map ID attribute            ap_tree :: APAttackTree attribute label,
   }                                              configuration :: Conf attribute
                                            }
```

A B.Bimap is a dictionary where we can efficiently look up IDs given a label or efficiently look up labels given an ID. A M.Map is a typical dictionary, and () is the unit type.

This design has several benefits. Internal attack trees are very easy to translate to various backends, especially formulas because we can use the IDs on base attacks as atomic formulas – which has its own benefits discussed below – and modifying labels and attributes is more efficient than having them labeled on the trees themselves. The previous data types reveal that actually all attack trees are attributed process attack trees, and a process attack tree simply does not use the attributes. This allows Lina to offer a uniform syntax for specifying all types of attack tree.

One important aspect of the definition of the various forms of attack trees is that the types label and attribute are actually type variables, and thus, our definition of attack trees is very general; in fact, label and attribute can be instantiated with any type whose elements are comparable. This property is captured by ad-hoc polymorphism using type classes in Haskell, and is checked during type checking.

Conducting threat analysis using attack trees requires them to be associated with an attribute domain. Typically, an attribute domain is a set, together with operations for computing the attribute of the branching nodes of an attack tree given attributes on the base attacks. In Lina attribute domains are defined by a type, here called attribute, and a configuration:

```
data Conf attribute = (Ord attribute) => Conf {
  orOp  :: attribute -> attribute -> attribute,
  andOp :: attribute -> attribute -> attribute,
  seqOp :: attribute -> attribute -> attribute
}
```

Utilizing higher-order functions we can define configurations easily and generically. For example, here is the configuration that computes the minimum attribute for choice nodes, the maximum attribute for parallel nodes, and takes the sum of the children nodes as the attribute for sequential nodes:

```
minMaxAddConf :: (Ord attribute,Semiring attribute) => Conf attribute
minMaxAddConf = Conf min max (.+.)
```

Notice here that this configuration will work with any type at all whose elements are comparable and form a semiring, thus making configurations generic and reusable. This includes types like Integer and Double.

The definitional language for attributed process attack trees of type APAttackTree attribute label is described by the following grammar:

```
at ::= base_na label | base_wa attribute label | or_node label at1 at2
     | and_node label at1 at2 | seq_node label at1 at2
```

```
import Lina.AttackTree

vehicle_attack :: APAttackTree Double String
vehicle_attack = start_PAT $
  or_node "Autonomous Vehicle Attack"
    (seq_node "External Sensor Attack"
      (base_wa 0.2 "Modify Street Signs to Cause Wreck")
      (and_node "Social Engineering Attack"
        (base_wa 0.6 "Pose as Mechanic")
        (base_wa 0.1 "Install Malware")))
    (seq_node "Over Night Attack"
      (base_wa 0.05 "Find Address where Car is Stored")
      (seq_node "Compromise Vehicle"
        (or_node "Break In"
          (base_wa 0.8 "Break Window")
          (base_wa 0.5 "Disable Door Alarm/Locks"))
        (base_wa 0.1 "Install Malware")))
```

Fig. 3. Lina Script for an Autonomous Vehicle Attack.

A full example of the definition of an attributed process attack tree for attacking an autonomous vehicle can be found in Fig. 3. The definition of `vehicle_attack` begins with a call to `start_PAT`. Behind the scenes, all of the ID's within the internal attack tree are managed implicitly, which requires the internals of Lina to work within a special state-based type. The function `start_PAT` initializes this state. Finally, we can define the vehicle attack tree as follows:

```
vehicle_AT :: AttackTree Double String
vehicle_AT = AttackTree vehicle_attack minMaxMaxConf
```

This attack tree associates the vehicle attack attributed process attack tree with a configuration called `minMaxMaxConf` that simply takes the minimum as the attribute of choice nodes, and the maximum as the attribute of every parallel and sequential node. Lina as two important features that other tools lack. First, it can abstract the definitions of attack trees. Second, it is highly compositional, because it is embedded inside of a functional programming language. Consider the following abstraction of `vehicle_attack`:

```
vehicle_AT' :: Conf Double -> AttackTree Double String
vehicle_AT' conf = AttackTree vehicle_attack conf
```

Here the configuration has been abstracted. This facilitates experimentation because the security practitioner can run several different forms of analysis on the same attack tree using different attribute domains. Attack trees in Lina can also be composed and decomposed; hence, complex trees can be broken down into smaller ones, then studied in isolation. This helps facilitate correctness, and offers more flexibility. As an example, in Fig. 4 we break up `vehicle_attack` into several smaller attack trees. We can see in the example that if we wish to

```se_attack :: APAttackTree Double String```
 ```se_attack = start_PAT $```
 ``` and_node "social engineering attack"```
 ```   (base_wa 0.6 "pose as mechanic")```
 ```   (base_wa 0.1 "install malware")```
	```bi_attack :: APAttackTree Double String```
	 ```bi_attack = start_PAT $```
	 ``` or_node "break in"```
	 ``` (base_wa 0.8 "break window")```
	 ``` (base_wa 0.5 "disable door alarm/locks")```

```cv_attack :: APAttackTree Double String```
 ```cv_attack = start_PAT $```
 ``` seq_node "compromise vehicle"```
 ```   (insert bi_attack)```
 ```   (base_wa 0.1 "install malware")```
	```es_attack :: APAttackTree Double String```
	 ```es_attack = start_PAT $```
	 ``` seq_node "external sensor attack"```
	 ``` (base_wa 0.2 "modify street signs to cause```
	 ``` wreck")```
	 ``` (insert se_attack)```

```on_attack :: APAttackTree Double String```
 ```on_attack = start_PAT $```
 ``` seq_node "overnight attack"```
 ```   (base_wa 0.05 "Find address where car```
 ```   is stored")```
 ```   (insert cv_attack)```
	```vehicle_attack'' :: APAttackTree Double String```
	 ```vehicle_attack'' = start_PAT $```
	 ``` or_node "Autonomous Vehicle Attack"```
	 ``` (insert es_attack)```
	 ``` (insert on_attack)```

Fig. 4. The autonomous vehicle attack decomposed

use an already defined attack tree in an attack tree we are defining, then we can make use of the **insert** function. As we mentioned above, behind the scenes Lina maintains a special state that tracks the identifiers of each node; thus, when one wishes to insert an existing attack tree, which will have its own identifier labeling, into a new tree, then that internal state must be updated; thus, **insert** carries out this updating. Lina is designed so that the user never has to encounter that internal state. So far we have introduced Lina's basic design and definitional language for specifying causal attack trees, and we have already begun seeing improvements over existing tools; however, Lina has so much more to offer. We now introduce Lina's support for reasoning about and performing analysis on causal attack trees. Kordy et al. [8] introduce the SPTool, an equivalence checker for causal attack trees that makes use of the rewriting logic system Maude [3] which allows one to specify rewrite systems and systems of equivalences. Kordy et al. specify the equivalences for causal attack trees from Jhawar et al.'s [6] work in Maude, and then use Maude's querying system to automatically prove equivalences between causal attack trees. This is a great idea, and we incorporate it into Lina, but we make several advancements over SPTool. Lina includes a general Maude interface, and allows the user to easily define new Maude backends, where a *Maude backend* corresponds to a Maude specification of a particular rewrite system. Currently, Lina has two Maude backends: equivalences for causal attack trees, and the multiplicative attack tree linear logic (MATLL). The former is essentially the exact same specification as the SPTool, but the latter corresponds to the two quaternary logics defined in Sect. 3. Attributed process attack trees are converted into the following syntax:

$$\text{(Maude Formula) } F := \text{ID} \mid F1; F2 \mid F1.F2 \mid F1 + F2$$

```
mod MATLL is
  protecting LOOP-MODE .
  sorts Formula .
  subsort Nat < Formula .
  op _||_  : Formula Formula -> Formula [ctor assoc comm] .
  op _._  : Formula Formula -> Formula [ctor assoc comm prec 41] .
  op _;_  : Formula Formula -> Formula [ctor assoc prec 40] .
  var a b c d : Formula .
  rl [a1]        : a . (b || c)      => (a . b) || (a . c) .
  rl [a1Inv]     : (a . b) || (a . c) => a . (b || c) .
  rl [a2]        : a ; (b || c)      => (a ; b) || (a ; c) .
  rl [a2Inv]     : (a ; b) || (a ; c) => a ; (b || c) .
  rl [a3]        : (b || c) ; a      => (b ; a) || (c ; a) .
  rl [a3Inv]     : (b ; a) || (c ; a) => (b || c) ; a .
  rl [a4]        : (a . b) ; c       => a . (b ; c) .
  rl [a4Inv]     : a . (b ; c)       => (a . b) ; c .
  rl [a5]        : (a ; b) . (c ; d) => (a . c) ; (b . d) .
  rl [a5Inv]     : (a . c) ; (b . d) => (a ; b) . (c ; d) .
  rl [switch]    : a ; (b . c)       => b . (a ; c) .
  rl [seq-to-para] : a ; b           => a . b .
endm
```

Fig. 5. Maude specification for MATLL.

This is done by simply converting the internal attack tree into the above syntactic form. For example, the Maude formula for the autonomous vehicle attack from Fig. 3 is (0 ; (1 . 2)) || (5 ; ((6 || 7) ; 2)), where each integer corresponds to the identifier of the base attacks. Note that the base attack 2 appears twice, this is because this base attack appears twice in the original attack tree. This syntax is then used to write the Maude specification for the various backends. The full Maude specification for the causal attack tree equivalence checker can be found in Appendix A. However, Kordy et al.'s specification only supports proving equivalences, but what about specializations? Lina supports proving specializations between attack trees using the MATLL Maude backend. Its full Maude specification can be found in Fig. 5. The axioms a1 through a5 are actually equivalences, but the last two rules are not. At this point we can use these backends to reason about attack trees. The programmer can make queries to Lina by first importing one or more Lina modules, and then making a query using Haskell's REPL – read, evaluate, print, loop – called GHCi. Consider the example Lina program in Fig. 6. These are the attack trees from Fig. 2. Then an example Lina session is as follows:

```
> :load source/Lina/Examples/Specializations.hs
...
Ok, modules loaded
> is_specialization enc_data2 enc_data1
True
>
```

In this session we first load the Lina script from Fig. 6 which is stored in the file Specializations.hs. Then we ask Lina if enc_data2 is a specialization of enc_data1, and Lina responds True, thus automating the proof given in Example 1. In addition to reasoning about attack trees, Lina also support analysis of

```
import Lina.AttackTree
import Lina.Maude.MATLL
-- A
enc_data1 :: PAttackTree String
enc_data1 = start_PAT $
  and_node "obtain secret"
    (or_node "obtain encrypted file"
      (base_na "bribe sysadmin")
      (base_na "steal backup"))
    (seq_node "obtain password"
      (base_na "break into system")
      (base_na "install keylogger"))

-- C
enc_data2 :: PAttackTree String
enc_data2 = start_PAT $
  or_node "obtain secret"
    (and_node "obtain secret via sysadmin"
      (base_na "bribe sysadmin")
        (seq_node "obtain password"
          (base_na "break into system")
          (base_na "install keylogger")))
    (seq_node "break in, then obtain secret"
      (base_na "break into system")
      (and_node "obtain secret from inside"
        (base_na "install keylogger")
        (base_na "steal backup")))
```

Fig. 6. Full Lina script for the attack trees A and C from Fig. 2.

attack trees. Currently, Lina supports several types of analysis: evaluating attack trees, querying the attack tree for the attribute value of a node, projecting out the set of attacks from an attack tree, and computing the maximal and minimal attack. When one defines an attack tree that tree is left unevaluated; that is, the attribute dictionary associated with the attack tree only has attributes recorded for the base attacks. If one wishes to know the attribute values at the branching nodes, then one must evaluate the attack tree, which populates the attribute dictionary with the missing attributes. For example, we may evaluate the attack tree for the autonomous vehicle attack from Fig. 3, and query the tree for the attributes at various nodes:

```
> let (Right e_vat) = eval vehicle_AT
> e_vat <@> "social engineering attack"
0.6
>
```

Here we first evaluate the attack tree `vehicle_AT` giving it the name `e_vat`, and then we use the attributed query combinator `<@>` to ask for the attribute at the parallel node labeled with `"social engineering attack"`. Note that the evaluator, `eval`, uses the configuration associated with the attack tree to compute the values at each branching node. It is also possible to project out various attacks from an attack tree. In Lina an *attack* corresponds to essentially an attack tree with no choice nodes. We call its data type `Attack attribute label`. An attack does not have any choice nodes, because they are all split into multiple attacks; one for each child node. For example, the set of possible attacks for the autonomous vehicle attack from Fig. 3 can be found in Fig. 7. Lina can compute these automatically using the `get_attacks` command. Finally, given the set of attacks for the autonomous vehicle attack we can also compute the set of minimal and maximal attacks. For example, consider the following session:

```
> min_attacks.get_attacks $ vehicle_AT
[SEQ("over night attack",0.5)
("Find address where car is stored",0.05)
(SEQ("compromise vehicle",0.5)
("disable door alarm/locks",0.5)
("install malware",0.1))]
```

```
SEQ("external sensor attack",0.6)
        ("modify street signs to cause wreck",0.2)
        (AND("social engineering attack",0.6)
                ("pose as mechanic",0.6)
                ("install malware",0.1))
```

```
SEQ("over night attack",0.8)
        ("Find address where car is stored",0.05)
        (SEQ("compromise vehicle",0.8)
                ("break window",0.8)
                ("install malware",0.1))
```

```
SEQ("over night attack",0.5)
        ("Find address where car is stored",0.05)
        (SEQ("compromise vehicle",0.5)
                ("disable door alarm/locks",0.5)
                ("install malware",0.1))
```

Fig. 7. Set of possible attacks for an autonomous vehicle attack.

In this session we first apply `get_attacks` to `vehicle_AT` to compute the set of possible attacks, and then we compute the minimal attack from this set.

5   Conclusion and Future Work

We made two main contributions: a new four-valued truth table semantics of causal attack trees that supports specializations of attack trees, and a new embedded domain specific programming language called Lina for specifying, reasoning, and analyzing attack trees.

We plan to investigate completeness results with respect to the ideal and filterish quaternary logics. Lina is under active development, and we have a number of extensions planned, for example, adding support for attack-defense trees, attack(-defense) graphs, attack nets, a GUI for viewing the various models, and a SMT backend. Finally, it is necessary for number of case studies to be carried out within Lina to be able to support the types of analysis required for real world applications.

Acknowledgments. This work was supported by NSF award #1565557. We thank Clément Aubert for helpful discussions and feedback on previous drafts of this paper, and the anonymous reviewers whose recommendations made this a better paper.

A   Maude Specification for Causal Attack Trees

```
mod Causal is

protecting LOOP-MODE .

sorts Formula .
subsort Nat < Formula .

op _||_    : Formula Formula -> Formula [ctor assoc comm] .
op _._     : Formula Formula -> Formula [ctor assoc comm] .
op _;_     : Formula Formula -> Formula [ctor assoc] .
op EQ(_,_) : Formula Formula -> Bool .

var P Q R S : Formula .

eq P . (Q || R)  = (P . Q)  || (P . R) .
eq P ; (Q || R)  = (P ; Q)  || (P ; R) .
eq (Q || R) ; P  = (Q ; P)  || (R ; P) .

ceq EQ(P,Q) = true
  if P = Q .
eq EQ(P,Q) = false .

endm
```

References

1. Camtepe, S.A., Yener, B.: Modeling and detection of complex attacks. In: Security and Privacy in Communications Networks, pp. 234–243, September 2007
2. Claessen, K., Hughes, J.: Quickcheck: a lightweight tool for random testing of haskell programs. SIGPLAN Not. **46**(4), 53–64 (2011)
3. Clavel, M., Durán, F., Eker, S., Lincoln, P., Martı-Oliet, N., Meseguer, J., Talcott, C.: Maude manual (version 2.1). SRI International, Menlo Park (2005)
4. Gadyatskaya, O., Trujillo-Rasua, R.: New directions in attack tree research: catching up with industrial needs. In: Liu, P., Mauw, S., Stølen, K. (eds.) GraMSec 2017. LNCS, vol. 10744, pp. 115–126. Springer, Cham (2018). https://doi.org/10.1007/978-3-319-74860-3_9
5. Horne, R., Mauw, S., Tiu, A.: Semantics for specialising attack trees based on linear logic. Fundam. Inform. **153**(1–2), 57–86 (2017)

6. Jhawar, R., Kordy, B., Mauw, S., Radomirović, S., Trujillo-Rasua, R.: Attack trees with sequential conjunction. In: Federrath, H., Gollmann, D. (eds.) SEC 2015. IAICT, vol. 455, pp. 339–353. Springer, Cham (2015). https://doi.org/10.1007/978-3-319-18467-8_23

7. Jones, S.P.: Haskell 98 Language and Libraries: The Revised Report. Cambridge University Press, Cambridge (2003)

8. Kordy, B., Kordy, P., van den Boom, Y.: SPTool - equivalence checker for SAND attack trees. In: Cuppens, F., Cuppens, N., Lanet, J.-L., Legay, A. (eds.) CRiSIS 2016. LNCS, vol. 10158, pp. 105–113. Springer, Cham (2017). https://doi.org/10.1007/978-3-319-54876-0_8

9. Kordy, B., Mauw, S., Radomirović, S., Schweitzer, P.: Foundations of attack–defense trees. In: Degano, P., Etalle, S., Guttman, J. (eds.) FAST 2010. LNCS, vol. 6561, pp. 80–95. Springer, Heidelberg (2011). https://doi.org/10.1007/978-3-642-19751-2_6

10. Kordy, B., Pouly, M., Schweitzer, P.: Computational aspects of attack–defense trees. In: Bouvry, P., Kłopotek, M.A., Leprévost, F., Marciniak, M., Mykowiecka, A., Rybiński, H. (eds.) SIIS 2011. LNCS, vol. 7053, pp. 103–116. Springer, Heidelberg (2012). https://doi.org/10.1007/978-3-642-25261-7_8

11. Kordy, B., Pouly, M., Schweitzer, P.: A probabilistic framework for security scenarios with dependent actions. In: Albert, E., Sekerinski, E. (eds.) IFM 2014. LNCS, vol. 8739, pp. 256–271. Springer, Cham (2014). https://doi.org/10.1007/978-3-319-10181-1_16

12. Mauw, S., Oostdijk, M.: Foundations of attack trees. In: Won, D.H., Kim, S. (eds.) ICISC 2005. LNCS, vol. 3935, pp. 186–198. Springer, Heidelberg (2006). https://doi.org/10.1007/11734727_17

13. McDermott, J.P.: Attack net penetration testing. In: Proceedings of the 2000 Workshop on New Security Paradigms, NSPW 2000, pp. 15–21. ACM, New York (2000)

14. Norell, U.: Dependently typed programming in AGDA. In: Proceedings of the 4th International Workshop on Types in Language Design and Implementation, TLDI 2009, pp. 1–2. ACM, New York (2009)

15. Piètre-Cambacédès, L., ouissou, M.: Beyond attack trees: dynamic security modeling with Boolean logic driven Markov processes (BDMP). In: 2010 European on Dependable Computing Conference (EDCC), pp. 199–208, April 2010

16. Schneier, B.: Attack trees: modeling security threats. Dr. Dobb's J. **24**, 21–29 (1999)

17. Vazou, N., Seidel, E.L., Jhala, R., Vytiniotis, D., Peyton-Jones, S.: Refinement types for haskell. SIGPLAN Not. **49**(9), 269–282 (2014)

The Attacker Does not Always Hold the Initiative: Attack Trees with External Refinement

Ross Horne[1], Sjouke Mauw[2], and Alwen Tiu[3(✉)]

[1] CSC, University of Luxembourg, Esch-sur-Alzette, Luxembourg
`ross.horne@uni.lu`
[2] CSC/SnT, University of Luxembourg, Esch-sur-Alzette, Luxembourg
`sjouke.mauw@uni.lu`
[3] Research School of Computer Science, Australian National University, Canberra, Australia
`alwen.tiu@anu.edu.au`

Abstract. Attack trees provide a structure to an attack scenario, where disjunctions represent choices decomposing attacker's goals into smaller subgoals. This paper investigates the nature of choices in attack trees. For some choices, the attacker has the initiative, but for other choices either the environment or an active defender decides. A semantics for attack trees combining both types of choice is expressed in linear logic and connections with extensive-form games are highlighted. The linear logic semantics defines a specialisation preorder enabling trees, not necessarily equal, to be compared in such a way that all strategies are preserved.

Keywords: Attack trees · Linear logic · Extensive-form games · Game semantics

1 Introduction

An attack tree is a rooted labelled tree profiling the goals of an attacker. The use of AND-OR trees for security modelling dates back to 1999, when Schneier proposed attack trees as a simple and comprehensive way of representing security scenarios and to allow for their quantitative analysis [36]. Since 1999, numerous extensions of attack trees have been proposed. They augment the original model with additional refinement operators [7,25,27] or support not only offensive but also defensive behaviour [9,30,35]. An exhaustive overview of the existing attack tree-based models can be found in [31].

In most established semantics for attack trees, notably a semantics based on multisets [33], there is an implicit assumption that the attacker always has the initiative. This worst case scenario for the defender is a realistic assumption in traditional security scenarios, where the configuration of defensive measures is typically static. This implicit assumption gives the attacker the advantage

© Springer Nature Switzerland AG 2019
G. Cybenko et al. (Eds.): GraMSec 2018, LNCS 11086, pp. 90–110, 2019.
https://doi.org/10.1007/978-3-030-15465-3_6

that, whenever there is a choice to make between different avenues of attack, the attacker has sufficient knowledge to control such choices.

In the interest of security, allowing the attacker to always retain the initiative is undesirable. The defender may take the initiative by being aware of design decisions affecting the security risk of a system; minimising the risk by pro-actively closing down more damaging avenues of attack. Avenues can be closed down by active policy choices, for example avoiding outdated operating systems without ASLR; or inspecting workspaces to ensure sensitive information is not left unattended. One of several more sophisticated ways of addressing this problem is by Moving Target Defence [26], proposed, in a federal plan, as a methodological approach to security breaking the asymmetry of the game between the attacker and defender. Instead of the system defences being static, while the attacker holds the advantage of being able to constantly adapt, the system defences can also constantly change. Such constant changes can result in situations where the attacker has insufficient knowledge to make an optimal choice. As a further example, consider honey pots, where, by directing a potentially malicious software to a sandbox, a network of defenders learns information about a network of attackers rather than vice versa. Such pro-active and adaptive defence policies can be categorised as intrusion tolerant approaches to system security [17].

As a simple policy scenario, where the initiative shifts in the favour of the defender, consider for example the attack tree in Fig. 1 adapted from the first attack-defence tree to appear in the literature [36]. The tree consists of goals that are disjunctively refined, indicated by the branching of the tree. A disjunctively refined node indicates that one of several sub-goals should be achieved in order for the attacker to succeed in its goal. For example, to open the safe the attacker can choose one of the sub-goals "pick lock", "cut open safe" or "learn combo". For now we assume the attacker has the initiative for this decision, hence is able to try any of these three options.

Now, in contrast to the root node, consider the node "learn combo", which is disjunctively refined into "find written combo" and "get combo from target". The question is whether the attacker has the luxury to resolve this choice. We can say that this is a choice, but, arguably, a choice that is external to the attacker. Suppose that managers take a proactive decision to counter this risk, assessing that an attacker finding a combo written by an employee is not only a serious risk but one that can be made unlikely by a clear company policy and security inspections of the workplace. Thus an action such as "find written combo" is an opportune event that, by policy, can be made more difficult for the attacker to achieve. Later, new data may arrive, perhaps for a foreign branch office, suggesting having employees susceptible to subversion is the greatest risk; a risk that can also be dynamically countered by a pro-active policy decisions by the defender, aware of the range of possible attacks.

We annotate the node "learn combo" with a box □ to indicate that there is a choice; but, by system design, a choice external to the attacker. The box notation has several connotations: firstly, a box suggests the choice is treated as a black box inside which the attacker cannot access; secondly, a box is typically

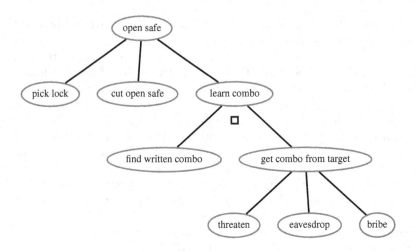

Fig. 1. Attack tree for opening a safe.

used for the external choice operator in models of concurrency [11]; thirdly, for readers familiar with modal logic, there is a connection with the box modality in the sense that the attacker must be prepared for all possible branches that may arise, assuming, for external choices, the attacker does not know which branches will be made unlikely by defensive measures.

The box suggests a simple extension of the methodology for using attack trees as a tool for security risk analysis and system design. Given an attack tree representing the potential attacks on a system, we observe each node where a choice is made and ask the question: "can the system be designed, e.g., by company guidelines or a moving target defence policy, such that the attacker does not have sufficient knowledge to make an optimal choice?"

Identifying some choices as external to the attacker, subtly changes the quantitative analysis performed over an attack tree. For example, in the attack tree adapted from Schneier, marking one node as external will never benefit the attacker—the damage of an attack may be reduced and the cost to the attacker may increase. By comparing the result of risk analysis with and without the node marked as external we can assess the impact of concentrating resources on a policy decision. We may wish to discover, for example, the percentage increase in cost to the attacker incurred by a policy decision. For example, without any pro-active policy, we may assess that the cheapest attack is to "find a written combo" at the cost of $10 k outlay to the attacker. However, with a policy avoiding the cheapest attack by which the combo can be learnt in the running example, we may assess that if the cheapest option the attacker can choose is to cut open the safe at the cost of $12 k, then we can conclude there is a 20% increase in the cost to the attacker. This assessment is of course dependant on data available on the attack scenario.

The presence of external choices also demands a more refined semantics that distinguishes moves by the attacker and the attacker's external environment. Sometimes the environment is the defender, but external choice may model uncertainty inherent in the environment the attacker operates. The semantics of external choices becomes particularly interesting when considering the notion of "specialisation" [25] introduced for comparing attack trees that are not necessarily equivalent. This paper introduces several semantics for attack trees: a minimal extension of the standard multiset semantics [33]; a novel game semantics [3,16,29]; and semantics based on linear logic [21]. Our use of the game semantics is particularly novel since it reconnects a branch of game theory arising from the study of logic with quantitative game theory. We find that the linear logic semantics preserves optimal strategies.

Outline. Section 2, for clarity, begins with a minimal attack tree model with disjunctive refinement only. The section lays down a case for a semantics with specialisation and how specialisation exposes the need for external refinement. The semantics of external refinement is explored from the perspectives of sets. Section 3 expands on the model in the previous section from the perspective of game semantics and logic.

Remark on Conjunctive Refinement. Attack trees feature both conjunctive and disjunctive refinement. However, this paper concerns only disjunctive refinement. This choice is made for pedagogical reasons—to explore the new feature of external refinement in a minimal setting. All semantics introduced in this paper can be extended with conjunctive refinement, following the use of the multiplicative connectives of linear logic in related work [25].

2   Specialisation for Attack Trees with Disjunctive Refinement

This section considers a minimal fragment of the attack tree notation in which we can explain the subtlety between choices that an attacker makes and choices where the attacker does not necessarily have the power to make decisions.

Central to this development are the notion of *action refinement*, the refinement of basic actions into attack trees consisting of several actions, and *specialisation* [25]. Attack trees are expected to evolve as new attacks are considered, or larger attack trees are pruned down to just the relevant actions. In such scenarios, a specialisation order can be used to ensure that certain properties are preserved by the specialisation, e.g., quantitative attribute values associated with two trees are correlated in some way.

2.1   Attack Trees with Disjunctive Refinement only

We begin with perhaps the simplest possible attack tree model—attack trees with disjunctive refinement only. Such trees consist of *basic actions* representing goals of an attacker, such as "disrupt network" or "kill node", and nodes that are *disjunctively refined* into sub-goals. For example the first tree in Fig. 2, disjunctively refines "disrupt database", by indicating at least one of "disrupt network" or "kill node" should be achieved.

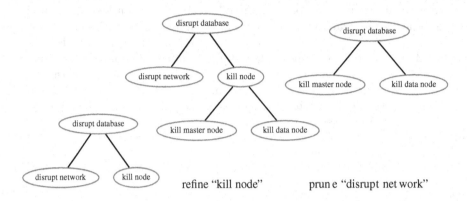

refine "kill node"   prun e "disrupt net work"

Fig. 2. Three attack trees: the middle tree obtained from the tree on the left by *action refinement*; the third tree on the right a *specialisation* of the tree in the middle.

A central idea in the attack tree methodology is *action refinement*. For example, "kill node" can be refined disjunctively to "kill master node" or "kill data node". This action refinement transforms the first tree in Fig. 2 to the second tree.

Perhaps the simplest semantics is to interpret each basic node as a singleton set and disjunction using union (the labels at nodes are just helpful annotations). Note this is semantically equivalent to the established multiset semantics [33] in this simplified scenario where there are no conjunctive nodes. Conjunctive refinement, representing when multiple sub-goals should all be achieved in order to achieve a goal (essentially an attack vector) is omitted. We know how to reintroduce conjunctive refinement into this model at a later stage, but we focus this study on choices only.

Under this set semantics, the first two trees in Fig. 2 are interpreted simply by the following sets.

first tree: { "disrupt network", "kill node" }
second tree: { "disrupt network", "kill master node", "kill data node" }

Notice that the sets are different hence the trees are neither equivalent in this simple semantics.

Now consider the third tree in Fig. 2, which is also clearly not equivalent to the second tree in Fig. 2. However, for any interpretation of basic actions as sets those trees are related by subset inclusion, as follows.

{ "kill master node", "kill data node" }
        ⊆ { "disrupt network", "kill master node", "kill data node" }

In this situation, where trees are related by subset inclusion, we say the tree with the smaller denotation *specialises* the other.

Specialisation has several useful applications in the attack tree methodology. Typically an attack tree is not a fixed static specification. It evolves as domain knowledge is added to the tree, or knowledge is pruned from the tree to focus on the relevant part of an attack [34]. In some use cases, multiple trees can be combined to model a more complex system. In other use cases, differences between two attack trees for the same scenario but generated by different agents may need to be reconciled, while showing the semantics of one or more attack trees is reflected in the combined tree. Previously the idea of specialisation has been explicitly explored in the setting of attack trees with sequential refinement [25].

2.2   Distinguishing Disjunctive from External Refinement Using a Box Annotation

We extend attack trees by allowing disjunctive refinement to be annotated with a box. Consider the attack tree in Fig. 3, differing from the second attack tree in Fig. 2 only with respect to the box annotation.

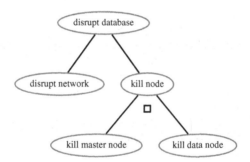

Fig. 3. Attack tree with a node labelled as external.

The box annotation indicates that the choice between the two sub-goals, namely "kill master node" and "kill data node", is external to the attacker and is instead made by the environment or an implicitly modelled defender of the system. To give a concrete scenario, the attacker can choose between setting out to disrupt the network or kill a node. However, we assume that the system has been designed such that the attacker cannot reliably distinguish between master nodes and data nodes hence, in the sub-tree "kill node", does not have the luxury to choose. Throughout this work we assume the limit case where the attacker must assume the worst case scenario for the attacker, implicitly by an active defender stacking the odds against the attacker.

Notice that this scenario suggests that there is an implicit system design decision at that point. This, we claim, can be used to model the impact of a policy decision in the system design, such as a moving target defence strategy, explicitly built into the configuration of the network to keep the defender guessing—breaking the asymmetry between the attacker and defender.

To help understand the impact of annotating a node as external consider the notion of an attribute domain [33]. An attribute domain simply determines a way of propagating quantities through attack trees. For example, we might want to calculate the maximum damage (in the running scenario, say seconds of downtime) the attacker can induce according to an attack tree. Calculations are performed with respect to a valuation mapping basic actions to values, such as the following.

"disrupt network" $\mapsto 20,$ "kill master node" $\mapsto 100,$ "kill data node" $\mapsto 2$

If we consider the central attack tree in Fig. 2, without the box annotation, the maximum damage, in the previous section, is simply the maximum of all values assigned to basic actions, i.e., maximum damage 100 s downtime.

The difference with the same attack tree with the box annotation, in Fig. 3, is that the external refinement is interpreted by minimum. Recall a moving target defence strategy has been explicitly implemented to make the more damaging outcome unlikely. Thus, under the same valuation, for the same tree but with the box annotation, the maximum damage is calculated to $\max\{20, \min\{100, 2\}\}$, i.e. maximum damage 20 s downtime.

More subtly, observe that the 20 s of downtime corresponds to the situation where the attacker decides to take the action "disrupt network". This choice can be explained in term of a game between two players—the attacker and its environment (sometimes, but not always, an active defender). The attacker aims to achieve maximum damage, while the environment aims to minimise damage. Initially the attacker has two choices, between "disrupt network" and the sub-tree named "kill node". However, the sub-tree "kill node" consists of two alternatives "kill master node" and "kill data node" that are in control of the environment. A perfect play for the environment (or defender) in the sub-tree "kill node", is to play the least damaging option. For the above example valuation, the least damaging option is "kill data node". Thus the optimal strategy for the attacker is to play the action "disrupt network", since if it plays the sub-tree "kill node" then the defender can be assumed to take the least damaging option "kill data node", resulting in less damage than 20 s downtime.

In the above example, the attacker has imperfect information about some moves in the game. In particular, those moves annotated with a box. Furthermore, for any valuation, the attribute domain gives the same answer as the game explanation, e.g., changing "kill data node" to damage 300, will result in an optimal play, where the attacker selects sub-tree "kill node" then the defender chooses "kill master node" resulting in a damage of 100 s downtime. The next sections make the underlying *game semantics* precise.

Note, given sufficient data, alternatively such scenarios can be modelled probabilistically, where uncertainty in the environment does not exclude the worst option, only making it less likely. This can lead to more precise results. However, we argue the approach of simply identifying external choices, is simpler, since no data on probabilities is required. Furthermore, all data has inherent uncertainty, hence risk analysis can at best provide ballpark figures. For example, the high level information a risk analyst is likely to appreciate from the analysis in this section is, as follows: "the proposed moving target defence policy, can result in reducing database down time from an attack by up to 80% (20 s downtime rather than 100 s)". Such an improvement would likely sway the security policy of an organisation.

2.3   A Distributive Lattice Semantics Covering External Refinement

Perhaps the simplest semantics that we can use to make the intuition of external choice precise is based on distributive lattices. In order to define a suitable distributive lattice model of attack trees (still without conjunctive refinement), we follow a standard construction for free finite distributive lattices, due to Birkhoff [8]. We require a function, the prime-irreducible closure π, that maps any finite non-empty set to its greatest prime-irreducible subsets. A prime-irreducible set is simply a set W such that if $x, y \in W$ then neither $x \subseteq y$ nor $y \subseteq x$. Thereby only maximal sets are recorded in the prime-irreducible closures, for example $\pi(\{\{a\}, \{a, b\}\}) = \{\{a, b\}\}$.

Each basic action is interpreted as a prime-irreducible set, external refinement is interpreted as the prime-irreducible closure of the union of two sets, while disjunctive refinement is interpreted by the prime-irreducible closure of the point-wise union of sets of sets, where point-wise union is defined as follows:

$$V + W = \{x \cup y \colon x \in V, y \in W\}$$

In order to discuss disjunctive attack trees, it is convenient to have the following grammar.

$$
\begin{aligned}
t &:= a & \text{basic actions} \\
&\mid t \triangledown t & \text{disjunctive refinement (as in standard attack trees)} \\
&\mid t \,\square\, t & \text{external refinement (nodes annotated with } \square\text{)}
\end{aligned}
$$

Basic actions record the labels at the leaves of attack trees, such as "disrupt network". Note labels at nodes, when attack trees are represented graphically, are not recorded in this grammar, since they are generally treated implicitly; although recent work has also considered grammars where the labels at nodes are remembered during tree transformations [20].

Definition 1. *The "distributive lattice semantics" is defined by the following mapping, where ϑ is any valuation mapping basic actions to non-empty prime-irreducible sets.*

$$I_\vartheta^{dl}(a) = \vartheta(a) \qquad I_\vartheta^{dl}(t \,\square\, u) = \pi\left(I_\vartheta^{dl}(t) \cup I_\vartheta^{dl}(u)\right) \qquad I_\vartheta^{dl}(t \triangledown u) = \pi\left(I_\vartheta^{dl}(t) + I_\vartheta^{dl}(u)\right)$$

Note it is standard in model theory to consider all interpretations of atoms, as achieved by the considering all mapping ϑ in the above semantics. From an attack tree perspective considering all interpretations, has the effect of ensuring the semantics is robust under all possible action refinements (replacing of basic actions by more complex attack trees). This issue is less significant for attack trees with disjunctive refinement, but becomes significant for extension of this model, e.g., where conjunctive refinement and external refinement co-exist. Thus we adopt a good model-theoretic practices to facilitate extensions.

In this distributive lattice model, based on certain sets of sets, the outer level set lists the choices that the environment has, while the inner level sets list the choices that the attacker has after the environment chose one set from the outer level set. The distributive lattice specialisation preorder is defined as follows.

Definition 2 (distributive lattice specialisation). *Given two disjunctive attack trees t and u, t specialises u, written $t \preceq u$ whenever, for all valuations ϑ, and for all $y \in I_{\vartheta}^{dl}(u)$, there exists $x \in I_{\vartheta}^{dl}(t)$ such that $x \subseteq y$. I.e., every set in the denotation of u covers some set in the denotation of t.*

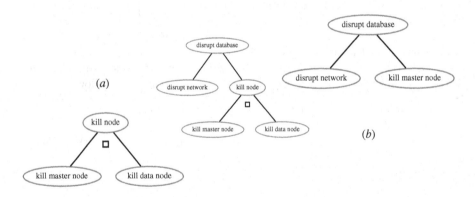

Fig. 4. Three attack trees related by distributive lattice specialisation: the attacker has the least advantage in the tree (a), and the greatest advantage in tree (b). The tree in Fig. 3 lies between these trees.

According to the above definition the trees in Fig. 4 are related by specialisation. The trees in this figure have the following respective denotations, under one possible valuation $\vartheta($ "kill master node" $) \mapsto \{\{master\}\}$, $\vartheta($ "kill data node" $) \mapsto \{\{data\}\}$, and $\vartheta($ "disrupt network" $) \mapsto \{\{network\}\}$. The central denotation in this chain is for the tree in both Figs. 3 and 4.

Fig. 4(a) $\{\{master\}, \{data\}\} \preceq \{\{network, master\}, \{network, data\}\}$ Fig. 3
$\preceq \{\{network, master\}\}$ Fig. 4(b)

The above inequalities hold under any possible valuation ϑ mapping basic actions to non-empty prime-irreducible sets.

Observe, under the maximum damage attribute domain and example valuation defined in previous sections, the maximum damage increases from left to right according to the specialisation order. For the trees in Figs. 4(a), 3 and 4(b), the maximum damage is respectively 2 s, 20 s and 100 s downtime. Furthermore, we know that for any valuation the same inequalities will be preserved.

The above observations leads us to the following **compatibility criterion**:

An attribute domain is *compatible* with a specialisation relation whenever for all pairs of trees related by specialisation, there is a correlation between the values at the root of the trees, for any assignment of values to basic actions at the leaves.

The above is a criterion, not a definition, that can be instantiated with any notion of attack tree, specialisation and correlation. The following is a definition specific to disjunctive attack trees and preorders for specialisation and correlation.

Definition 3. *An attribute domain for disjunctive attack trees* $\mathcal{D} = (D, f, g)$ *is given by domain D ordered by $\leq$, where f and g are binary operators. The interpretation in that domain is defined as follows, for any valuation ϑ mapping basic actions to D:*

$$I_\vartheta^{\mathcal{D}}(a) = \vartheta(a) \qquad I_\vartheta^{\mathcal{D}}(t \triangledown u) = f(I_\vartheta^{\mathcal{D}}(t), I_\vartheta^{\mathcal{D}}(u)) \qquad I_\vartheta^{\mathcal{D}}(t \square u) = g(I_\vartheta^{\mathcal{D}}(t), I_\vartheta^{\mathcal{D}}(u))$$

An attribute domain $\mathcal{D}$ is compatible with a specialisation $\preceq$, whenever for all attack trees t and u such that $t \preceq u$, and all valuations ϑ, we have $I_\vartheta^{\mathcal{D}}(t) \leq I_\vartheta^{\mathcal{D}}(u)$.

A concrete example of an attribute domain compatible with the distributive lattice semantics is the maximum damage attribute domain used in examples so far $(\mathbb{N}, \min, \max)$. Further examples include attribute domains based on classical propositional logic and de Morgan algebras (e.g. three value logic indicating low, medium and high risk). The product of distributive lattices is a distributive lattice. Thus, multi-parameter attribute domains [5,12,28], such as the product of the maximum damage attribute domain and an attribute domain indicating whether an attack is possible using classical propositional logic, are also compatible with the distributive lattice semantics.

In the next section, we observe that the distributive lattice semantics is simply a way of representing normal form games.

3   A Game Semantics for Disjunctive Attack Trees

As suggested informally, for examples presented so far, the interplay between disjunctive and external refinement, respectively choices made by the attacker and the environment of the attacker, can be considered as an extensive-form game. An extensive-form game is described as a tree of choices annotated to indicate whether the proponent or opponent makes the choice—where the proponent and opponent are respectively the attacker and its environment (or defender) in the setting of disjunctive attack trees. Extensive-form games can be seen as a natural

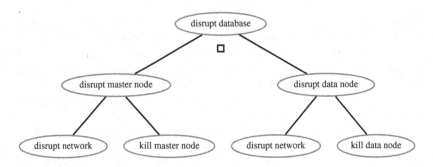

Fig. 5. An attack tree equivalent under the distributive lattice semantics to the tree in Fig. 3; but strictly more generous to the attacker under two-player simulation (Definition 4).

extension of the distributive lattice semantics, preserving more structure about the knowledge of the attacker and defender at various points in the game.

To see how the distributive lattice semantics forgets some of the structure of an extensive-form game consider the tree in Fig. 5, which has the following denotation, identical to the denotation of the tree in Fig. 3: $\{\{network, master\}, \{network, data\}\}$, considered under the previously described mapping of basic actions to non-empty prime-irreducible sets: $\vartheta($ "kill master node" $\mapsto \{\{master\}\}$, $\vartheta($ "kill data node" $\mapsto \{\{data\}\}$, and $\vartheta($ "disrupt network" $\mapsto \{\{network\}\}$.

If we consider only the optimal strategy for the games, it is fine to consider the trees in Figs. 3 and 5 to be equivalent. In the optimal strategy for the tree in Fig. 5 the defender gets to move first, and will ensure that the least damaging choice is taken—the sub-tree labelled "disrupt data node" under the running example valuation. In the sub-game "disrupt data node", the attacker chooses "disrupt network" or "kill data node", taking the most damaging option—"disrupt network" according our running attribute domain. This gives the same result, 20 s downtime—the same answer as for the optimal game on the tree in Fig. 3.

An explanation for why the two attack trees described are equivalent is that optimal strategies pick out the minimal and maximal strategies, depending on which player holds the initiative. Minimum and maximum distribute over each other, hence an extensive-form game can always be normalised into a game where both players simultaneously declare their optimal position—a normal form game. If we consider disjunctive attack trees to be extensive-form games, then the distributive lattice semantics can be regarded as capturing the normal forms of such games. In such a setting, the main argument for permitting extensive-form games is data-structures for extensive form game may be exponentially smaller than for normal-form games.

3.1 Sub-optimal Strategies and a Games Semantics for Disjunctive Attack Trees

A subtle argument for preserving the structure of play in an attack tree, based on semantics, is we may desire to preserve not just the meaning of optimal strategies, but also suboptimal strategies, where one player makes a suboptimal choice, or dually a lucky choice. Consider the trees in Figs. 3 and 5 as extensive-form games, presented syntactically by the respective terms related by the inequality below.

$$network \bigtriangledown (master \,\square\, data) \precsim (network \bigtriangledown master) \,\square\, (data \bigtriangledown network)$$

We can say that the tree on the left can be *simulated* (notation: $\precsim$) by the tree on the right as follows. If the attacker chooses "disrupt network" (abbreviated *network*) on the left, "disrupt network" is still enabled for the attacker on all paths on the right. If the attacker chooses $master \,\square\, data$ on the left, then for all paths the defender can choose in $(network \bigtriangledown master) \,\square\, (data \bigtriangledown network)$, there is a corresponding path for the defender on the left where *master* is enabled and another path where *data* is enabled.

Notice the switching from the attacker to the defender and back in the informal explanation of the above example. This two-player simulation game can be defined by the following coinductive definition.

Definition 4 (two-player simulation). *Given a disjunctive attack tree t, the moves of the attacker $t \Longrightarrow^A t'$ are given by all terms t' reachable from t by maximal sequences of rewrites of the form $t_1 \bigtriangledown t_2 \longrightarrow t_i$, where $i \in \{1, 2\}$ (or $t \Longrightarrow^A t$ if there is no such transition). Dually, the moves of the defender $t \Longrightarrow^D t'$ are given by terms t' reachable by maximal sequences of transitions of the form $t_1 \,\square\, t_2 \longrightarrow t_i$, where $i \in \{1, 2\}$ (or $t \Longrightarrow^D t$ if there is no such transition).*

A two-player simulation $\mathcal{R}$ is a relation between attack trees such that, whenever $t \,\mathcal{R}\, u$ the following hold:

- *If $t \Longrightarrow^A t'$ and $u \Longrightarrow^D u'$ then there exist t'' and u'' such that $t' \Longrightarrow^D t''$ and $u' \Longrightarrow^A u''$ and $t'' \,\mathcal{R}\, u''$.*
- *If neither player can move in either tree, t and u are the same basic action.*

We say a tree t is simulated by u, written $t \precsim u$ whenever there exists a two-player simulation $\mathcal{R}$ such that $t \,\mathcal{R}\, u$.

Example of Two-Player Simulation. Consider again the running example. To verify $network \bigtriangledown (master \,\square\, data) \precsim (network \bigtriangledown master) \,\square\, (data \bigtriangledown network)$ holds, observe the pair is contained in a two-player simulation $\mathcal{S}$ containing the following pairs.

$$network \bigtriangledown (master \,\square\, data) \; \mathcal{S} \; (network \bigtriangledown master) \,\square\, (data \bigtriangledown network)$$
$$master \; \mathcal{S} \; master \qquad network \; \mathcal{S} \; network \qquad data \; \mathcal{S} \; data$$

To see that the above relation is a two-player simulation consider the four initial moves:

1. Consider when the attacker moves in the first tree to *network* and the defender moves in the second tree to *network* $\triangledown$ *master*. This pair of moves can be matched by the move *network* $\triangledown$ *master* $\Longrightarrow^A$ *network*, reaching the pair *network* $\mathcal{S}$ *network*.
2. The case where the attacker moves to *network* in the first and defender moves to *data* $\triangledown$ *network* in the second is similar to the first case.
3. The attacker moves to *master* $\square$ *data* in the first tree and the defender moves to *network* $\triangledown$ *master* is the second tree. This pair of moves can be matched by transitions *master* $\square$ *data* $\Longrightarrow^D$ *master* in the first tree and *network* $\triangledown$ *master* $\Longrightarrow^A$ *master* in the second tree. Since *master* $\mathcal{S}$ *master* we are done.
4. The final case, where the attacker moves to *master* $\square$ *data* in the first tree and the defender moves to *network* $\triangledown$ *master* is the second tree, is similar to the third case.

Each pair in the simulation can be considered as a reachable pair of sub-games. In each pair of sub-games, optimal strategies remain correlated, even if a player made a sub-optimal choice in order to reach that sub-game. To see this, consider all sub-games, in the relation $\mathcal{S}$ under any distributive attribute domain and any valuation. The value, e.g., maximum damage, on the left is always less than or equal to the value on the right.

Another way to understand the two-player simulation intuitively is that the attacker plays according to the first board, while the defender plays according to the second board. If the actual attack scenario is the first board the defender can still perform its defences, and, symmetrically, if the actual attack scenario is the second board the attacker can still perform its attack. This indicates that in the first board, the attacker may be more restricted than in the second board, and, symmetrically, in the second board the defender may be more restricted than in the first board.

Stated in other terms: no matter what happens, the attacker can always be at least as effective in the attack tree on the right of a 2-player simulation relation, i.e., according to the tree in Fig. 5 in the running example, rather than the tree in Fig. 3.

A Counter-Model for a Two-Player Simulation. In contrast, there is no two-player simulation in the opposite direction. That is (*network* $\triangledown$ *master*) $\square$ (*data* $\triangledown$ *network*) is not simulated by *network* $\triangledown$ (*master* $\square$ *data*). To see why, observe initially the attacker cannot move in the first tree, nor can the defender move in the second tree. This identity initial move can be followed up by four possible moves to chose from.

1. In this first case, *master* $\triangledown$ *network* is not simulated by *network*, since if the attacker makes the move *master* $\triangledown$ *network* $\Longrightarrow^A$ *master*, this cannot be matched by *network*.
2. In the second case, for reasons similar to the first case, *data* $\triangledown$ *network* is not simulated by *network*.
3. In the third case, *network* $\triangledown$ *master* is not simulated by *master* $\square$ *data*. To see why, observe that if the attacker makes move *network* $\triangledown$ *master* $\Longrightarrow^A$ *master*

and the defender makes move $master \,\square\, data \Longrightarrow^D data$, clearly $master$ and $data$ are not equal in all models.

4. In the fourth case, for reasons similar to the third case, $network \,\triangledown\, data$ is not simulated by $master \,\square\, data$.

The above reasoning is independent of any valuation in a particular attribute domain. The above reasoning is satisfied by any semantics compatible, according to compatibility criterion, with respect to the specialisation relation defined by two-player simulation. However, we can give a concrete counter-model explained below.

If we consider a multi-parameter attribute domain, for example the product of maximum damage and whether an attack is possible, we can see that in each of the four cases above there is a valuation where the attacker has the initiative on the left but cannot maintain the initiative on the right. In concrete terms, consider the following valuation:

$$network \mapsto (5, false), \quad master \mapsto (20, false) \quad data \mapsto (5, true)$$

We can now calculate the optimal strategy using this distributive attribute domain and valuation in each of the four cases above. We get the following inequalities for the respective cases.

1. For $master \,\triangledown\, network$ and $network$, we have $(20, false) > (5, false)$.
2. For $data \,\triangledown\, network$ and $network$, we have $(5, true) > (5, false)$.
3. For $network \,\triangledown\, master$ and $master \,\square\, data$ we have $(20, false) \neq (5, true)$.
4. For $network \,\triangledown\, data$ and $master \,\square\, data$ we have $(5, true) \neq (20, false)$.

Thus in none of the pairs of sub-games enumerated, is it the case that the valuation on the left is less than or equal to the valuation on the right. Thus the correlation between the optimal strategies is broken in the sub-games.

An Example Specialising Disjunctive Refinement to External Refinement. As another example, observe the tree $network \,\triangledown\, (master \,\square\, data)$, from Fig. 3, is simulated by tree $network \,\triangledown\, master \,\triangledown\, data$ where external refinement is relaxed to disjunctive refinement, i.e., the middle tree in Fig. 2.

Initially, the attacker moves in the first tree to reach either $network$ or $master \,\square\, data$. In response to the former move, $network$ can be matched by a move by the attacker on the second tree to $network$. The later move can be matched by the defender making move $master \,\square\, data \Longrightarrow^D master$ in the first tree and the attacker making the move $master \,\square\, data \Longrightarrow^A master$ in the second tree. Thus the relation $\mathcal{T}$, defined as follows, is a two-player simulation.

$$network \,\triangledown\, (master \,\square\, data) \;\mathcal{T}\; network \,\triangledown\, master \,\triangledown\, data$$
$$network \;\mathcal{T}\; network \qquad\qquad master \;\mathcal{T}\; master$$

Next we provide a proof system where implication coincides with simulation.

3.2   Specialisation Expressed Using Additive Linear Logic

We provide a brief introduction to the additive fragment of linear logic [21], which is used to logically characterise 2-player simulation on disjunctive attack trees. A proof system for additive linear logic, ALL, is given in Fig. 6. Rules are expressed in the sequent calculus, where a *sequent*, of the form $\vdash \Delta$, where Δ is a multiset of propositions (thus permitting comma separated formulae to *exchange* position).

Linear negation, indicated by an overline, is a synthetic operator distinct from classical negation. *Additive* disjunction, $P \oplus Q$ (called "plus"), has a De Morgan dual additive conjunction, $P \& Q$ (called "with"), such that $\overline{P \& Q} = \overline{P} \oplus \overline{Q}$ and $\overline{P \oplus Q} = \overline{P} \& \overline{Q}$. All negations can be pushed to the atomic propositions a where $\overline{\overline{a}} = a$.

$$\frac{}{\vdash \overline{a}, a} \; axiom \qquad \frac{\vdash P_i, \Delta}{\vdash P_1 \oplus P_2, \Delta} \; \oplus, \, i \in \{1, 2\} \qquad \frac{\vdash P, \Delta \quad \vdash Q, \Delta}{\vdash P \& Q, \Delta} \; \&$$

Fig. 6. A sequent calculus for Additive Linear Logic.

If we desire to prove that P implies Q, written $P \multimap Q$, we search for a proof of the sequent $\vdash \overline{P}, Q$. For example, the axiom states that a basic action specialises itself. Also, the following is a proof of showing that *with* ($\&$) distributes in one direction over *plus* ($\oplus$), i.e. $a \oplus (b \& c) \multimap (a \oplus b) \& (a \oplus c)$.

$$\frac{\dfrac{\dfrac{}{\vdash \overline{a}, a} \, axiom}{\vdash \overline{a}, a \oplus b} \oplus \quad \dfrac{\dfrac{}{\vdash \overline{a}, a} \, axiom}{\vdash \overline{a}, a \oplus c} \oplus}{\vdash \overline{a}, (a \oplus b) \& (a \oplus c)} \& \qquad \dfrac{\dfrac{\dfrac{\dfrac{}{\vdash \overline{b}, b} \, axiom}{\vdash \overline{b}, a \oplus b} \oplus}{\vdash \overline{b} \oplus \overline{c}, a \oplus b} \oplus \quad \dfrac{\dfrac{\dfrac{}{\vdash \overline{c}, c} \, axiom}{\vdash \overline{c}, a \oplus c} \oplus}{\vdash \overline{b} \oplus \overline{c}, a \oplus c} \oplus}{\vdash \overline{b} \oplus \overline{c}, (a \oplus b) \& (a \oplus c)} \&}{\vdash \overline{a} \& (\overline{b} \oplus \overline{c}), (a \oplus b) \& (a \oplus c)} \&$$

The linear implication $(a \& b) \oplus (a \& c) \multimap a \& (b \oplus c)$ also holds by a similar proof. However, take care that, unlike classical logic which defines a distributive lattice, the converse implications do not hold. Thus linear logic preserves more structure regarding how operators are nested, as required to preserve the sub-games of an extensive-form game explained in the previous section.

We now define a linear logic semantics by using the following embedding of disjunctive attack trees as propositions in additive linear logic.

$$[\![t \triangledown u]\!] = [\![t]\!] \oplus [\![u]\!] \qquad [\![t \,\square\, u]\!] = [\![t]\!] \& [\![u]\!] \qquad [\![a]\!] = a$$

In this semantics, specialisation is defined by the provable linear implications. For example, by the proof above we have the following specialisation.

$$[\![network \triangledown (master \,\square\, data)]\!] \multimap [\![(network \triangledown master) \,\square\, (data \triangledown network)]\!]$$

Notice that the above example was already established by two-player simulation $\mathcal{S}$ in the previous section.

As another example, we have the following implication.

$$[\![network \triangledown (master \,\square\, data)]\!] \multimap [\![network \triangledown master \triangledown data]\!]$$

This implication, demonstrating a specialisation between attack trees, is verified by the following proof in the sequent calculus.

$$
\cfrac{
\cfrac{
\vdash \overline{network}, network
}{
\vdash \overline{network}, network \oplus (master \oplus data)
}\; axiom
\quad \oplus \quad
\cfrac{
\cfrac{
\cfrac{
\cfrac{
\vdash \overline{master}, master
}{
\vdash \overline{master}, master \oplus data
}\; axiom
}{
\vdash \overline{master} \oplus \overline{data}, master \oplus data
}\; \oplus
}{
\cfrac{
\vdash \overline{master} \oplus \overline{data}, network \oplus (master \oplus data)
}{
\vdash \overline{master} \oplus \overline{data}, network \oplus (master \oplus data)
}\; \oplus
}\; \oplus
}{
\vdash \overline{network} \,\&\, \left(\overline{master} \oplus \overline{data}\right), network \oplus (master \oplus data)
}\; \&
$$

The above proof also corresponds to a two-player simulation presented previously.

Logically speaking, the following theorem is a soundness and completeness result, checking, for any disjunctive attack tree, there is a correspondence between provable implications and two-player simulations.

Theorem 1. *Given disjunctive attack trees t and u, $\vdash [\![t]\!] \multimap [\![u]\!]$ if and only if $t \precsim u$.*

The above theorem follows from the soundness and completeness of an established game semantics for ALL [16]. Two-player simulation is simply a reformulation of ALL games directly on attack trees. The proof involves a more refined but equivalent *multi-focussed* [4,13] proof system for ALL, from which strategies are extracted.

Recall that two-player simulation preserves optimal strategies in all subgames. The following proposition follows, since the distributive lattice semantics preserves the optimal strategy for the main game tree, which is obviously also a sub-game.

Proposition 1. *Given disjunctive attack trees t and u, if $t \precsim u$ then $t \preceq u$.*

As demonstrated previously using Figs. 3 and 5, the distributive semantics does not preserve sub-optimal strategies, hence the converse does not hold.

4 Related and Future Work

We highlight related work in two directions, both connecting games and attack trees.

Related Work on Multiplicative-Additive Games and Game Semantics. Connections between dialogue games and logic are as old as the study of logic itself. For linear logic, the pioneering work on games semantics, due to Blass [10], suffered from compositionality issues that were fixed for the multiplicative fragment [1]. For MALL, the first satisfactory model proposed is based on a "truly concurrent" game semantics [3] where both players may simultaneously be active in different parts of the arena in which the game is played. Game models for an "intuitionistic" restriction of MALL have been developed [32] based on the idea of focussing. Focussing [4], exploits the fact that during proof search, half the rules are "invertible" meaning there is no need to backtrack once a decision is made. The two-player simulations in this work are based on a "neutral" approach to game semantics [16] for MALL based on multi-focussing [13], which disposed of the "intuitionistic" restriction. We have recreated this game semantics directly over attack trees, leading to a more direct but, in the case of conjunctive refinement, less symmetric definition.

Previous work on specialisation [25] of attack trees with sequential refinement [27] employs an extension of linear logic, called MAV [24], modelling sequentiality using a non-commutative operator. Since MAV extends MALL, external refinement and sequential refinement can co-exists in MAV. Defining a game semantics for MAV however remains an open problem. Game semantics, distinct from MALL games, have been applied to other security problems [2,15,18]

Related Work on Game Theory Applied to Attack Trees. Models capturing a game-strategic interaction between the attacker and the defender in attack trees have been noted previously. In [29], for instance, a relation between the propositional semantics of attack-defence trees and two player, binary, zero-sum games has been established. It shows that the two models are equivalent, however this result only applies to the problem of the satisfiability of a security scenario. In [23], Hermanns et al. lift the zero-sum assumption and consider three-valued logic (undecided, won by the attacker, won by the defender) to analyse the security scenarios using attack-defence diagrams. Attack-defence diagrams represent a game between an attacker and a defender competing with each other to swing the game from 'undecided' to 'won' by one of them. These diagrams however, have much richer structure than ADTrees – they are directed graphs handling cyclic behaviours, and capture quantitative information as well as dependencies between actions.

Several other game-based approaches to analysing security scenarios modelled by attack trees. In [6], ADTrees are transformed into stochastic two-player game and probabilistic model checking techniques are used to answer questions on the probability of successful attacks, with respect to various constraints, such as time. Model checking, and more precisely timed automata and the Uppaal tool, has also been used for the analysis of ADTrees [19]. The particularity of this framework is that it assumes that the defender acts only once. At the very beginning of the scenario, he selects a set of possible countermeasures to be implemented and the objective of the analysis is to find the most optimal strategy (from the quantitative perspective) of the attacker in this fixed setting. Yet another approach based on two-player Stackelberg stochastic games has also been proposed [37]. Their analysis is based on converting attack-response tree to security games, in order to evaluate the effectiveness of intrusion tolerance engines.

Future work will illustrate the subtitles of models combining external refinement and conjunctive refinement. Future work also includes reconciling the semantics in the current paper with the above probabilistic approaches to games, with the objective of defining a notion of specialisation that preserves "mixed" strategies and probabilistic attribute domains. Probabilities can also be approached from the perspective of logic and game semantics [14].

5   Conclusion

The contribution of this paper is a minimal methodology for analysing the impact of a pro-active security policy where some choices are external to the attacker. External choices are modelled by annotating some disjunctive refinements in an attack tree with a box $\square$. The methodology is made precise by developing two semantics, formalising the key observation that breaking the asymmetry in attack scenarios exposes a game between moves by an attacker and its environment.

This paper highlights advantages particular to the semantics defined by an embedding in MALL. The semantics based on ALL, Fig. 6, admits a decidable specialisation preorder for comparing trees not necessarily equivalent, with $\mathcal{O}(mn)$ time-complexity [22], where m and n are the sizes of the two trees being compared. The specialisation preorder can be characterised (Theorem 1) by a game semantics (Definition 4) unfolding the extensive-form game underlying an attack tree, such that all strategies are preserved. Specialisation respects (Proposition 1) a more obvious semantics based on distributive lattices (Definition 2), preserving optimal strategies only. Recall that, without a semantics, attack trees can be interpreted differently by tools, possibly unpredictably affecting the quantitative analysis of attacks.

Acknowledgment. Horne and Tiu receive support from MOE Tier 2 grant MOE2014-T2-2-076 and the National Research Foundation Singapore under its National Cybersecurity R&D Program (Award No. NRF2014NCR-NCR001-30). Mauw received funding from the Fonds National de la Recherche Luxembourg, grant C11/IS/1183245 (ADT2P), and the European Commissions Seventh Framework Programme (FP7/2007–2013) under grant agreement number 318003 (TREsPASS).

References

1. Abramsky, S., Jagadeesan, R.: Games and full completeness for multiplicative linear logic. J. Symbolic Logic **59**(2), 543–574 (1994). https://doi.org/10.2307/2275407
2. Abramsky, S., Jagadeesan, R.: Game semantics for access control. In: Proceedings of the 25th Conference on Mathematical Foundations of Programming Semantics (MFPS 2009) Electronic Notes in Theoretical Computer Science, vol. 249, pp. 135–156 (2009). https://doi.org/10.1016/j.entcs.2009.07.088
3. Abramsky, S., Melliès, P.-A.: Concurrent games and full completeness. In: 14th Annual IEEE Symposium on Logic in Computer Science LICS, Trento, Italy, 2–5 July 1999, pp. 431–442. IEEE Computer Society (1999). https://doi.org/10.1109/LICS.1999.782638
4. Andreoli, J.-M.: Logic programming with focusing proofs in linear logic. J. Logic Comput. **2**(3), 297–347 (1992). https://doi.org/10.1093/logcom/2.3.297
5. Aslanyan, Z., Nielson, F.: Pareto efficient solutions of attack-defence trees. In: Focardi, R., Myers, A. (eds.) POST 2015. LNCS, vol. 9036, pp. 95–114. Springer, Heidelberg (2015). https://doi.org/10.1007/978-3-662-46666-7_6
6. Aslanyan, Z., Nielson, F., Parker, D.: Quantitative verification and synthesis of attack-defence scenarios. In: 2016 IEEE 29th Computer Security Foundations Symposium (CSF), pp. 105–119. IEEE Computer Society (2016). https://doi.org/10.1109/CSF.2016.15
7. Audinot, M., Pinchinat, S., Kordy, B.: Is my attack tree correct? In: Foley, S.N., Gollmann, D., Snekkenes, E. (eds.) ESORICS 2017. LNCS, vol. 10492, pp. 83–102. Springer, Cham (2017). https://doi.org/10.1007/978-3-319-66402-6_7
8. Birkhoff, G.: Rings of sets. Duke Math. J. **3**(3), 443–454 (1937). https://doi.org/10.1215/S0012-7094-37-00334-X
9. Bistarelli, S., Fioravanti, F., Peretti, P.: Defense trees for economic evaluation of security investments. In: First International Conference on Availability, Reliability and Security (ARES 2006), pp. 416–423. IEEE Computer Society (2006). https://doi.org/10.1109/ARES.2006.46
10. Blass, A.: A game semantics for linear logic. Ann. Pure Appl. Logic **56**(1), 183–220 (1992). https://doi.org/10.1016/0168-0072(92)90073-9
11. Brookes, S.D., Hoare, C.A.R., Roscoe, A.W.: A theory of communicating sequential processes. J. ACM **31**(3), 560–599 (1984). https://doi.org/10.1145/828.833
12. Buldas, A., Laud, P., Priisalu, J., Saarepera, M., Willemson, J.: Rational choice of security measures via multi-parameter attack trees. In: Lopez, J. (ed.) CRITIS 2006. LNCS, vol. 4347, pp. 235–248. Springer, Heidelberg (2006). https://doi.org/10.1007/11962977_19
13. Chaudhuri, K., Miller, D., Saurin, A.: Canonical sequent proofs via multi-focusing. In: Ausiello, G., Karhumäki, J., Mauri, G., Ong, L. (eds.) TCS 2008. IIFIP, vol. 273, pp. 383–396. Springer, Boston, MA (2008). https://doi.org/10.1007/978-0-387-09680-3_26
14. Danos, V., Harmer, R.S.: Probabilistic game semantics. ACM Trans. Comput. Logic (TOCL) **3**(3), 359–382 (2002). https://doi.org/10.1145/507382.507385
15. Debbabi, M., Saleh, M.: Game semantics model for security protocols. In: Lau, K.-K., Banach, R. (eds.) ICFEM 2005. LNCS, vol. 3785, pp. 125–140. Springer, Heidelberg (2005). https://doi.org/10.1007/11576280_10
16. Delande, O., Miller, D., Saurin, A.: Proof and refutation in MALL as a game. Ann. Pure Appl. Logic **161**(5), 654–672 (2010). https://doi.org/10.1016/j.apal.2009.07.017

17. Deswarte, Y., Blain, L., Fabre, J.C.: Intrusion tolerance in distributed computing systems. In: Proceedings of 1991 IEEE Computer Society Symposium on Research in Security and Privacy, pp. 110–121, May 1991. https://doi.org/10.1109/RISP.1991.130780

18. Dimovski, A.S.: Ensuring secure non-interference of programs by game semantics. In: Mauw, S., Jensen, C.D. (eds.) STM 2014. LNCS, vol. 8743, pp. 81–96. Springer, Cham (2014). https://doi.org/10.1007/978-3-319-11851-2_6

19. Gadyatskaya, O., Hansen, R.R., Larsen, K.G., Legay, A., Olesen, M.C., Poulsen, D.B.: Modelling attack-defense trees using timed automata. In: Fränzle, M., Markey, N. (eds.) FORMATS 2016. LNCS, vol. 9884, pp. 35–50. Springer, Cham (2016). https://doi.org/10.1007/978-3-319-44878-7_3

20. Gadyatskaya, O., Jhawar, R., Mauw, S., Trujillo-Rasua, R., Willemse, T.A.C.: Refinement-aware generation of attack trees. In: Livraga, G., Mitchell, C. (eds.) STM 2017. LNCS, vol. 10547, pp. 164–179. Springer, Cham (2017). https://doi.org/10.1007/978-3-319-68063-7_11

21. Girard, J.-Y.: Linear logic. Theoret. comput. Sci. 50(1), 1–101 (1987). https://doi.org/10.1016/0304-3975(87)90045-4

22. Heijltjes, W., Hughes, D.J.: Complexity bounds for sum-product logic via additive proof nets and petri nets. In: 30th Annual ACM/IEEE Symposium on Logic in Computer Science, LICS 2015, Kyoto, Japan, 6–10 July 2015, pp. 80–91. IEEE Computer Society (2015). https://doi.org/10.1109/LICS.2015.18

23. Hermanns, H., Krämer, J., Krčál, J., Stoelinga, M.: The value of attack-defence diagrams. In: Piessens, F., Viganò, L. (eds.) POST 2016. LNCS, vol. 9635, pp. 163–185. Springer, Heidelberg (2016). https://doi.org/10.1007/978-3-662-49635-0_9

24. Horne, R.: The consistency and complexity of multiplicative additive system virtual. Sci. Ann. Comput. Sci. 25(2), 245 (2015). https://doi.org/10.7561/SACS.2015.2.245

25. Horne, R., Mauw, S., Tiu, A.: Semantics for specialising attack trees based on linear logic. Fund. Inform. 153(1–2), 57–86 (2017). https://doi.org/10.3233/FI-2017-1531

26. Jajodia, S., Ghosh, A.K., Swarup, V., Wang, C., Wang, X.S.: Moving Target Defense: Creating Asymmetric Uncertainty for Cyber Threats, vol. 54. Springer, Heidelberg (2011). https://doi.org/10.1007/978-1-4614-0977-9

27. Jhawar, R., Kordy, B., Mauw, S., Radomirović, S., Trujillo-Rasua, R.: Attack trees with sequential conjunction. In: Federrath, H., Gollmann, D. (eds.) SEC 2015. IAICT, vol. 455, pp. 339–353. Springer, Cham (2015). https://doi.org/10.1007/978-3-319-18467-8_23

28. Jiang, R., Luo, J., Wang, X.: An attack tree based risk assessment for location privacy in wireless sensor networks. In: WiCOM, pp. 1–4 (2012). https://doi.org/10.1109/WiCOM.2012.6478402

29. Kordy, B., Mauw, S., Melissen, M., Schweitzer, P.: Attack–defense trees and two-player binary zero-sum extensive form games are equivalent. In: Alpcan, T., Buttyán, L., Baras, J.S. (eds.) GameSec 2010. LNCS, vol. 6442, pp. 245–256. Springer, Heidelberg (2010). https://doi.org/10.1007/978-3-642-17197-0_17

30. Kordy, B., Mauw, S., Radomirović, S., Schweitzer, P.: Attack-defense trees. J. Logic Comput. 24(1), 55–87 (2014). https://doi.org/10.1093/logcom/exs029

31. Kordy, B., Piètre-Cambacédès, L., Schweitzer, P.: DAG-based attack and defense modeling: don't miss the forest for the attack trees. C. S. Rev. 13–14, 1–38 (2014)

32. Laurent, O.: Polarized games. Ann. Pure Appl. Logic 130(1–3), 79–123 (2004). https://doi.org/10.1016/j.apal.2004.04.006

33. Mauw, S., Oostdijk, M.: Foundations of attack trees. In: Won, D.H., Kim, S. (eds.) ICISC 2005. LNCS, vol. 3935, pp. 186–198. Springer, Heidelberg (2006). https://doi.org/10.1007/11734727_17

34. Ray, I., Poolsapassit, N.: Using attack trees to identify malicious attacks from authorized insiders. In: di Vimercati, S.C., Syverson, P., Gollmann, D. (eds.) ESORICS 2005. LNCS, vol. 3679, pp. 231–246. Springer, Heidelberg (2005). https://doi.org/10.1007/11555827_14

35. Roy, A., Kim, D.S., Trivedi, K.S.: Attack countermeasure trees: towards unifying the constructs of attack and defense trees. Secur. Commun. Netw. 5(8), 929–943 (2012). https://doi.org/10.1002/sec.299

36. Schneier, B.: Attack trees. Dr. Dobb's J. 24(12), 21–29 (1999)

37. Zonouz, S.A., Khurana, H., Sanders, W.H., Yardley, T.M.: RRE: a game-theoretic intrusion response and recovery engine. IEEE Trans. Parallel Distrib. Syst. 25(2), 395–406 (2014). https://doi.org/10.1109/TPDS.2013.211

A State Machine System for Insider Threat Detection

Haozhe Zhang[(✉)], Ioannis Agrafiotis, Arnau Erola, Sadie Creese,
and Michael Goldsmith

Department of Computer Science, University of Oxford, Oxford, UK
{haozhe.zhang,ioannis.agrafiotis,arnau.erola,
sadie.creese,michael.goldsmith}@cs.ox.ac.uk

Abstract. The risk from insider threats is rising significantly, yet
the majority of organizations are ill-prepared to detect and mitigate
them. Research has focused on providing rule-based detection systems
or anomaly detection tools which use features indicative of malicious
insider activity. In this paper we propose a system complimentary to the
aforementioned approaches. Based on theoretical advances in describing attack patterns for insider activity, we design and validate a state-
machine system that can effectively combine policies from rule-based
systems and alerts from anomaly detection systems to create attack patterns that insiders follow to execute an attack. We validate the system
in terms of effectiveness and scalability by applying it on ten synthetic
scenarios. Our results show that the proposed system allows analysts to
craft novel attack patterns and detect insider activity while requiring
minimum computational time and memory.

Keywords: Insider threat · Tripwires · Attack patterns

1 Introduction

There is growing evidence suggesting that organisations face significant risks
from insider threats. According to the Breach Level Index 40% of the publicly
reported data breaches were attributed to insiders who either maliciously or accidentally caused harm to their organisations [8]. In a similar vein, a survey conducted by ISACA [23] demonstrated that roughly 60% of the cyber-attacks which
organisations experienced in 2014 were attributed to insiders threats. Beside the
increase in the number of insider attacks, the inner knowledge and legitimate
access to the systems, security practices and sensitive company data that insiders possess render these types of attacks the most costly [3,20,22], with reports
suggesting that average damage can exceeded seven million dollars [14].

The dire implications, the increase in frequency, as well as challenges in
detecting and mitigating these threats have attracted the interest of the research
community over the last 20 years. Research has focused on conceptualising
the problem of insider threat [10,17,19] and proposing anomaly detection systems [11,12,15,22]. On the other hand, large organisations and stakeholders

© Springer Nature Switzerland AG 2019
G. Cybenko et al. (Eds.): GraMSec 2018, LNCS 11086, pp. 111–129, 2019.
https://doi.org/10.1007/978-3-030-15465-3_7

involved in the defence and intelligence community have tried to mitigate the risk of insider threat by training investigators to determine when employees may become a risk and by forming transparent security policies [1, 26].

In this paper we propose a novel system which complements current approaches in insider threat detection and combines information from anomaly detection tools and security policies from rule-based systems. More specifically, our system provides a visual interface to security analysts that enables them to design and detect attack pattens which insiders follow. It utilises knowledge from theoretical works describing behaviours that may indicate insider activity [3], parses different types of logs to create attack graphs, provides alerts when an attack pattern is complete and outputs statistical data and visualisations that describe employees' activity on real time. We validate our system in ten synthetic scenarios and report our results regarding the effectiveness and efficiency of the detection system as well as its scalability.

In what follows, Sect. 2 reviews the literature on insider threat with focus on theoretical advances and implementations of anomaly detection system and Sect. 3 describes the system architecture and the methodology we followed to capture the requirements for our system. Section 4 presents the synthetic scenarios and discusses our results, while Sect. 5 concludes the paper.

2   Literature Review

Literature on insider threat can be dichotomised in theoretical works aiming to understand behavioural factors, identify attack patterns and create conceptual models, and in practical research where a variety of anomaly detection tools with different capabilities are proposed. Carnegie Mellon University were the pioneers in examining human aspects of insider threat. In the CERT project, they applied System Dynamics to examine a series of insider threat case studies [10, 17]. Their proposed framework comprises four broad categories of insider cases, namely Information Technology (IT) Sabotage, Intellectual Property (IP) theft, Data and Financial Fraud, and Espionage. For each category, further behavioural aspects are identified and critical paths which insiders tend to follow are revealed. Their comprehensive work led to a series of "Management and Education of the Risk of Insider Threat" (MERIT) studies where emphasis was placed on understanding how qualitative characteristics such as disgruntlement and dissatisfaction can be early indicators of insider threat activity [16].

Sarkar [24] provides a different perspective by distinguishing two classes of insiders, namely malicious and accidental. He identifies capability, motivation and opportunity as the three key factors which prompt insiders to act maliciously while human mistakes, errors, carelessness and bad design of the systems were the main characteristics of accidental insiders. In a similar vein, Nurse et al. examined a number of insider threat cases and developed a framework which describes not only technical or behavioural indicators but focuses on the motivation of the attackers as well [19]. Agrafiotis et al. analysed more than 100 cases of insider activity, identified unique atomic steps which insiders follow and reconstructed all the cases based on these steps. They examined the common steps in these cases and effectively revealed more than ten different attack patterns which insiders followed to execute their attack [3]. These attack patterns along with publicly available security policies are formalised in [1], where a grammar for insider threat detection is proposed.

Another strand of literature emphasises on designing practical solutions to detect insider threats. Such works utilise different machine learning techniques to create profiles of employees based on their digital activity and try to distinguish abnormal actions [5,15,18]. Parveen et al. [21] focus on streaming data and use unsupervised learning techniques to identify changes in employees behaviour over time, a concept which they coined as "concept-drift". Chen et al. [11] proposed a user-relationship network for identifying collaborative insider attacks and introduced an unsupervised learning framework, the Community-based Anomaly Detection System (CADS). The underlying algorithm is a combination of kNN and PCA. Buford et al. [9] examined the concept of situation awareness in the automatic insider threat detection by designing an agent-based approach able to simulate insider behaviour and potentially detect changes in behaviour patterns Brdiczka et al. [7], explored the use of psychological profiling to reduce the number of false positive alerts in detection systems. Another interesting approach used Bayesian networks to infer the behavioural attributes of users based on sentiment analysis on text and social network analysis [4]. Lastly, [27] presents an unsupervised anomaly detection method using an ensemble of individual detectors to identify unknown attacks. Authors assert they can achieve or even improve the same performance of detectors that tackle specific scenarios.

Our review of the literature suggests that there is no unified effort to bring together the conceptual models which consider human aspects, the rule-based models which capture security-policy violations and the anomaly detection tools. A system proposed in [2] considers all these elements but has validated only the anomaly detection engine. In this paper we address this gap by designing a system which is able to capture information for attack patterns as presented in [3] using as a framework the grammar presented in [1] which can formalise policy violations and attack patterns which include alerts from anomaly detection systems. By effectively filling this gap, we enable analysts to design and test known or novel attack patterns, obtain a holistic perspective of employees' behaviours in real time and prevent insider attacks before being utilised.

3   System Architecture and Implementation

The detection system proposed in this paper is a state machine model and follows the tripwire grammar defined in [1], which is a formal language to clearly and unambiguously describe policy violations and attack patterns. Due to the fact that these violations can be triggered by a single system log and that no previous knowledge of the users profile is required, they are coined as *tripwires*.

An attack pattern P, as the Fig. 1 shows, is a directed acyclic graph containing a finite number of *states* Σ and *transitions* Φ. Each transition is directed from one state to another, in such a way that there does not exist a consistently-directed sequence of transitions that starts from an arbitrary state σ and loops back to σ again. The states reflect the status of progress of P for a specific user and the transitions represent the attack steps that can be chosen from P. We use $S \in P$ and $\phi \in P$ to represent that the state S and the transition ϕ are in the pattern P.

Figure 1 shows an example of an attack pattern P describing an IP theft. The attack pattern captures the sequence of observed behaviour (observed behaviour is identified by parsing the necessary logs that organisations keep to monitor digital activity i.e., file logs, web logs, system logs within a specific time frame-work) and once complete (the S_4 state is reached) an alert is triggered. Formally, the attack pattern P is defined by the states $\Sigma_P = \{S_0, S_1, S_2, S_3, S_4\}$ and transitions $\Phi_P = \{\phi_0, \phi_1, \phi_2, \phi_3, \phi_4\}$ where S_i or ϕ_i represents a state or a transition with id i and belongs to attack pattern P. The $S_{from}, S_{to},$ *trigger* and *time* for any transition is defined below:

$$\phi_x : S_x \xrightarrow{<UserN,ActionY>,time} S_x + 1,$$

A key aspect of the transition that challenges the state machine model is the time within which a specific transition should be observed. The rationale behind being that an attack pattern must be executed within a specific time framework. It would be of no interest for example to observe a user accessing

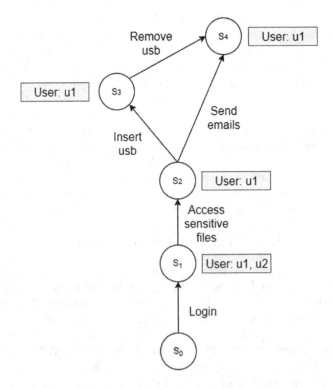

Fig. 1. The attacking progress of users u_1 and u_2

sensitive files and correlate this action to an email that is sent a month after. Once a completed attack is detected by the system, an alert is raised which comprises ⟨*user, time, trace*⟩; where *time* indicates when the attack happened and the trace is the sequence of attack steps committed by the user to complete the attack.

The proposed system allows analysts to create and edit attack patterns using an interface. It further enables analysts to match the organisation logs and alerts from detection systems to behaviours of interest as well as to monitor when there are accomplished by employees. The system parses the logs and tracks progress of all employees with respect to the created attack patterns in real-time and provides detailed statistics of the attacks through these interfaces. As Fig. 2 shows, our detection system comprises two parts: the *front-end* and the *back-end*. The front-end refers to the presentation layer focusing on providing user-friendly interfaces, while the back-end refers to the data access layer which handles the logic of the detection system and storage of data.

JavaScript is chosen as the primary programming language due to its highly increasing popularity for web based application developing. The community of JavaScript provides a powerful open-source libraries for building interfaces including D3.js [6] which is for creating dynamic, interactive data visualisations in browsers and React.js [13] which is for handling efficient updates of interfaces. The D3.js is applied for the construction of statistical charts in the interfaces, and the React.js is useful for the real-time update of the model monitor. The

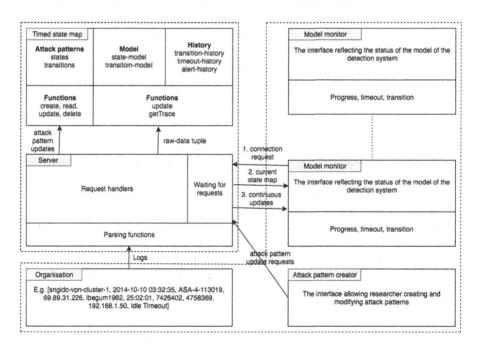

Fig. 2. The structure of state machine system

back end of detection system is developed using Node.js [25] which is an open source JavaScript run-time environment for executing JavaScript code server-side, while the front end interfaces are developed in HTML, CSS and JavaScript which can be executed by browsers.

We have designed the system with a modular approach meaning that the interfaces and subsystems are independent: they are encapsulated and have different duties. This was motivated by the fact that it is easier to modify the system to adapt to different datasets and attack patterns. We can modify or turn off one sub-system without changing others to meet different requirements. For example, when connecting a new organisation with a different log format, the system requires different parsing functions to translate the logs to the formatted inputs that can be recognised by the *timed state map*. The *timed state map* component maintains progress for attack patterns for every user. It is the subsystem server's duty to parse the logs, so we need to replace the old server with a new one which contains the specific parsing functions for the new organisation.

3.1   Main Components of the System

The system comprises three sub-models which are *state-model, transition-model* and *history*. The state-model and transition-model are defined as set of tuples which are named *state tuples* and *transition tuples* respectively, or s-tuple and t-tuple for short. The *history* comprises different types of tuples recording the history of processing raw logs. Storing every possible instantiation of an attack pattern for every employee is not feasible, as will lead to a state explosion. We create a single instance for every attack pattern per user and we aggregate in their graph all the necessary information and present the most advanced state. All actions are recorded and once the time frame for observing a transition has elapsed, the system is able to back track to the second most advanced state based on the historical data. This is achieved with the use of s-tuples and t-tuples.

More specifically, an s-tuple is the record indicating the state a user is at and it contains the components *user, state* and *time*; where the *time* indicates the time the user reaches this state. A t-tuple is the record of a transition commenced by a user and it contains the components *user, transition* and *time*. All users are in the initial states for all the attack patterns by default. A transition ϕ can be triggered by a user when the $\phi.S_{from}$ has already been reached by the user, and the user is carrying out the $\phi.trigger$ and satisfies the $\phi.time$. We name the set of states reached by a user the *territory* of the user and users can expand their territories on the attack patterns by triggering attack steps leading from the states in their territory to unoccupied states. Figure 1 shows the attack progress of users u_1 and u_2 with respect to the attack pattern P. The territory of u_1 is $\{S_0, S_1, S_2, S_3, S_4\}$ and the territory of u_2 is $\{S_0, S_1\}$.

The ***trace*** of an s-tuple s is defined as the sequence of history states the user $s.user$ has reached from the initial state S_0 to the $s.state$. For example, the trace of tuple $\langle u_1, S_4, time \rangle$ is $[S_0, S_1, S_2, S_3, S_4]$ and the trace of tuple $\langle u_2, S_1, time \rangle$ is $[S_0, S_1]$. We store the progress of a user in an attack pattern by keeping only one record for a state or transition in the attack pattern tree. Formally, this is ensured by the two *model-rules*:

1. at the certain time, a single state can be reached by a single user at most one time, i.e. there cannot be two s-tuples s_1 and s_2 such that $s_1.user = s_2.user \land s_1.state = s_2.state$.
2. at the certain time, a single transition can be commenced by a single user at most one time, i.e. there cannot be two t-tuples t_1 and t_2 such that $t_1.user = t_2.user \land t_1.S_{from} = t_2.S_{from} \land t_1.S_{to} = t_2.S_{to}$.

The history is used to keep track of the statistical information generated during the processing. This data is useful for the evaluation of the attack patterns and provides useful insights on common routes that attackers follow, allowing an analyst to act before the final steps of an attack are executed. The history of logs processed by the detection is shown in the *Processing Log* panel on the top left corner in Fig. 3.

To update the model, every time the system parses a log it matches it to the territory of the *user* which is all the states the *user* is currently in. Then, the system calculates all the transitions that the *user* can trigger based on the current state; this set of transitions is named *candidate transitions*: $\Phi_{candidate}$. Since each transition refers to only one attack step, we only need to consider the transitions extended from the territory, which means the transitions directed from the states occupied by the *user*, i.e. $\Phi_{candidate} = \{\phi \mid \phi \in \Phi, \phi.S_{from} \in S_{user}\}$.

Next, since the calculation of candidate transitions does not consider the triggering events and timeout constraints, we know $\Phi_{target} \subseteq \Phi_{candidate}$. So, we need to filter the $\Phi_{candidate}$ by applying the trigger and timeout constraints. Also, if a transition expires, we need to create a timeout event which represents a transition from the current state to S_0.

Once the set of target transitions is determined, we need to update the state-model, transition-model and history accordingly. For each timeout event $\phi_{timeout} \in \Phi_{target}$, we remove the s-tuple with value $\langle Tuple.user, \phi_{timeout}.S_{from}\rangle$ from the state-model which indicates that the user is no longer at the state and we add or update the timeout-history tuple with value $\langle Tuple.user, \phi_{timeout}, times\rangle$: if the tuple already exists, we set the initial *times* to one, else we increase *times* by one. Next, for each transition $\phi \in \Phi_{target}$, we add an s-tuple $\langle Tuple.user, \phi.S_{to}, Tuple.time\rangle$ and a t-tuple $\langle Tuple.user, \phi.S_{from}, \phi.S_{to}, Tuple.time\rangle$ to the state-model and transition-model. Similar to the timeout transition, we add or update the transition-history tuple with value $\langle Tuple.user, \phi, times\rangle$. According to the two model-rules introduced above, if there are s-tuples and t-tuples with the same $Tuple.user, \phi.S_{from}$ and $\phi.S_{to}$ values, we just update the time of the tuples without adding a new one. So, the model of the state map keeps only the latest behaviours of the users. Finally, when the output state is reached, i.e. $\phi_{S_{to}} \in \Sigma_f$, an alert-history tuple with value $\langle Tuple.user, trace, Tuple.time\rangle$ will be created and add to the history.

During the calculation of target transitions, all transitions should be commenced once the input raw-data tuple are parsed. However, there is a special case that there can be multiple transitions $\Phi_{duplicate}$ moving to the same state, i.e. $\Phi_{duplicate} \subseteq \Phi_{target}, s.t. \forall \phi_i, \phi_j \in \Phi_{duplicate}, \phi_i.S_{to} = \phi_j.S_{to}$. For this case, we remove other transitions and only leave a transition ϕ_{latest} which is directed from the state with the latest reaching time, i.e. $\phi_{latest} \in \{\forall \phi_i \in \Phi_{duplicate}, \phi_{latest}.S_{from}.time \geq \phi_i.S_{from}.time\}$. Note the ϕ_{latest} is selected randomly from the transitions directed from the latest occupied state and this ensures there will be at most one transition directed to a state at one time.

Removing some of the transitions in $\Phi_{duplicate}$ will change the resulting t-tuples but the result of s-tuples would not be affected because the ϕ_{latest} who has the same target state with removed transitions is persistent: the target state would be reached anyway, which means the upcoming updates would not be affected. Commencing only the ϕ_{latest} ensures the trace of an s-tuple is deterministic (can be represented by an array) and trace follows the latest behaviours.

Visual interfaces are the GUIs developed to allow researchers to access and manipulate the data of the state map, as well as to visualise statistics about attacks. Several visual interfaces with different functions are developed in this project.

The first visualisation of the interface is the *progress view*, which reflects the real-time progress of attacks for a selected attack pattern. Consider that the attack pattern *pattern2* is selected, as Fig. 3 shows; the attack pattern is shown by a DAG on the right of the interface. The s-tuples are reflected by labelling the users beside the states that they belong to. The size of a state S in the DAG reflects the number of users at S, i.e. a larger state means there are more users at S. The history of logs processed by the detection is shown in the *Processing Log* panel on the top left corner.

As Fig. 4 shows, the data for transitions are grouped by their transition id and presented by tables where vertical columns depict the number of times that the user commenced a transition. In addition, the interfaces provide a bar chart showing the comparison of frequencies of these transitions. The horizontal axis shows the transitions and different colours with different proportions in a bar refer to the number of times that the user commenced this transition. A DAG of a selected attack pattern is also provided, which reflects the frequencies of these transitions: the transitions with higher frequency have thicker links in the DAG. These views can reflect on design problems of the attack patterns, such as the interval time of a transition is too short or too long.

Alert view presents statistics on alerts that are flagged. With a similar interface as the transition view, the alerts are grouped by their traces and are represented in tables with columns named user and time as shown in Fig. 5a. The interface also provides a bar chart indicating the number of these alerts. In addition, by comparing the number and composition of different groups of alerts, analysts can get statistical results such as "which trace of a given attack pattern is more frequent" and "which employees are more likely to commit a given attack."

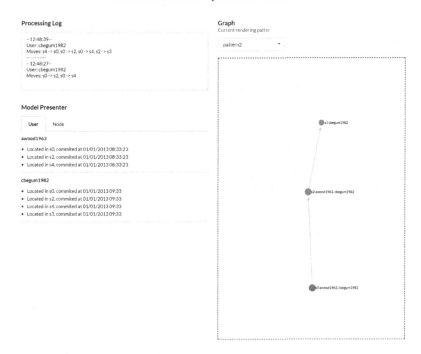

Fig. 3. The progress view of a model monitor

Pattern editor enables analysts to design and implement attack patterns in the state map, i.e. creating and modifying attack patterns through the buttons and input boxes without coding. The interface enables analysts to input the values for the attributes of Σ_P and Φ_P. These attributes are based on the data available and the system supports a predetermined number of attributes. The data that are currently supported are raw data from logs (file, web, email, login) and alerts from the CITD anomaly detection system. These alerts can be either unusual deviations from a normal behaviour or policy violations [2]. When special attributes are required it is straightforward to manually denote these into the parser module which will then update the pattern editor. Further details can be found in Appendix 1.C.

Log importer sends logs to the server so it can be considered as the *organisation* part shown in Fig. 2. As Fig. 5b shows, it allows analysts to edit and send test logs to the system. The *server* of the system will consume the logs and start processing them.

4   System Validation

We validate our system in terms of efficiency and scalability on ten synthetic scenarios. These scenarios were designed as part of the Corporate Insider Threat

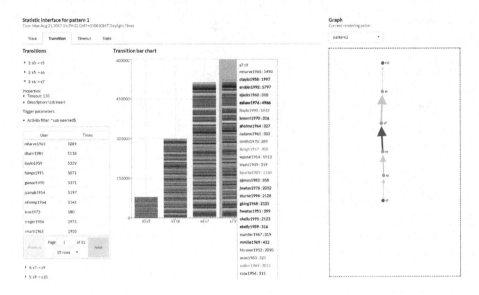

Fig. 4. The transition view of the model monitor (Color figure online)

(a) The table in the alert view   (b) Log importer

Fig. 5. The table in the alert view & log importer

Detection (CITD) project, which was sponsored by the UK National Cyber Security Programme in conjunction with the Centre for the Protection of National Infrastructure. The ground truth of these scenarios was made available to the authors only after all the results for all the scenarios was generated.

Each scenario contained login, file, website, email and usb activity logs for a period of one year (01/01/2013–31/12/2013), the number of employees varied from 12 to 300 and captured cases from IP theft to sabotage and financial gains. To evaluate the detection system, the attack patterns presented in [3] were implemented using the attack pattern editor interface. The system returned alerts on employees, indicating the paths of the attack which the employees followed and the time when the last step occurred. More details about the dataset for each scenario can be found in Appendix 1.A. The specific attack patterns with the time frameworks can be found in Appendix 1.B.

4.1   Efficiency of the System

Due to space limitations, we will present in detail the results and visual outputs from one scenario and we will discuss the overall effectiveness of the tool on the rest of the scenarios in Sect. 5. The chosen scenario describes a disgruntled software developer who had recently being offered a position in a rival company. The developer had then used their company email address to send source code files to their own personal webmail address. There are particular folders of interest in the file log data which start from the path /svn or /development. Only one attack pattern was triggered when we run the system that pertained to IP data exfiltration via email and indicated the perpetrator of the attack. The single and correct output alert in this scenario was $nricha1989$, $19/12/2013\ 19:25:03$, $S0->S1->S2->S3->S5->S6$.

Statistical data on transitions of all employees is shown in Fig. 6. The data of transitions on the left side of the image enable analysts to select a specific transition to identify its characteristics and the number of times this transition occurred. The bar chart on the right shows on the x axis the transitions and on y axis the number of times this transition occurred. The bars are coloured differently and each colour represents different employees in the organisation. Analysts can hoover over a bar to elicit further details. The transparency of the colour is proportional to the number of times this employee has triggered the transition.

From Fig. 6 we can see that the vast majority (over 95%) of transitions refer to the first two steps of the attack pattern which are login and access to sensitive files. Due to the fact that the number of transitions for the next states is rather small, the colour indicating their frequency is not visible in the figure but the number be retrieved from the statistical data. It is expected to observe an overwhelming number of transitions for the first two steps and an equally overwhelming number of time out events in Fig. 7 for these transitions. Employees login to the organisation's system to access files as part of their daily routine. They normally need to access multiple files, so the "sensitive file accessing" steps are more frequent than the "login" steps. The frequencies of the next steps in the progression of the attack pattern are much lower because the CITD system generated a small number of cmss alerts. The number of transitions to the next step is reduced to one. Only the insider cmss accessed an unusual volume of

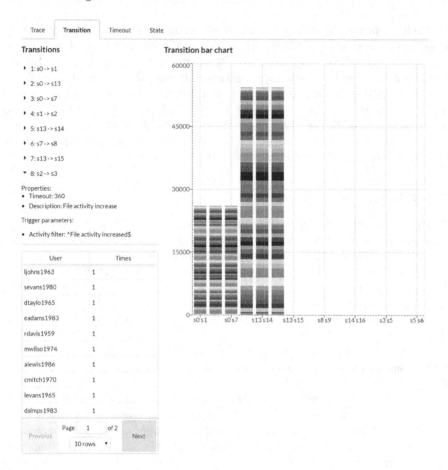

Fig. 6. The transition view of the scenario 1 (Color figure online)

files and sent emails with big attachments to their personal email address. This behaviour is denoted by the transitions cmss.

As Fig. 7 shows, setting appropriate time frameworks for the transitions between states is of paramount importance. In our case, most of the transitions after the first two steps expired because the employees did not proceed further. The timeout events ensured that reasonably short intervals, e.g. in within a day, are required for an attack to be accomplished. Our results here highlight how valuable a state machine system can be in insider threat detection. An anomaly detection system would only provide indicators of abnormal behaviour and would probably increase the number of false positive alerts. Furthermore, these systems tend to be oblivious to the sequence with which certain actions take place. When alerts from such systems are combined with alerts from rule-based tools then behavioural aspects of an attack can be inferred as shown in our example. Furthermore, it is possible for an analyst to intervene before the final step of an attack is executed and mitigate the harms for an organisation.

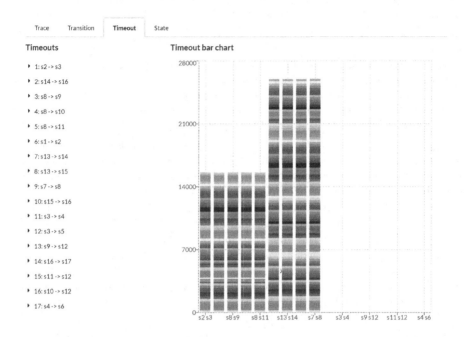

Fig. 7. The timeout view of the scenario 1 (Color figure online)

Similar conclusions can be drawn for all the other scenarios, where our system has generated no false positives but failed to identify the perpetrator in three scenarios. In all cases the frequency of the steps decrease exponentially the further we proceed in the attack pattern. This is an indication that the attack patterns presented in [3] effectively indicate insider activity. Furthermore, our system can complement an anomaly detections system as well as a rule-based tool and decrease the number of false positive alerts generated by these systems. On the other hand, the lack of an alert for three scenarios reveals that there is further work to be conducted in the design of attack patterns. The attacks in for the scenarios which the system did not generate an alert were subtle and the perpetrators were amongst the users who reached the higher states of certain attack patterns. We believe that the statistical data provided by our system can enable analysts to refine and tailor attack patterns to specific organisations. The key success criterion being that the more advanced the state is the less frequent its transitions should be.

4.2   Scalability of the System

Focusing on memory usage, the three components which are stored in memory are the state-model, the transition-model and the history. The sizes of the state and transition models are $O(|S|)$ and $O(|T|)$ respectively, where $|S|$ and $|T|$ are the number of states and transitions in the attack patterns. The complexity of the history is the sum of transition-history, alert-history and timeout-history. The size required by the alert-history is based on the number of logs. However, since the number of alerts raised by the detection system is fairly small, the memory required by the alert-history can be omitted. So, the space complexity of the history is $|transition - history| + |timeout - history| = O(2|T|)$. As the model maintains a behaviour profile for each user, by summing up the complexities calculated above, the space complexity of the detection system is $O(|U|(3|T| + |S|))$, where $|U|$ is the number of employees in the organisation.

The rather small complexity is due to the fact that the system does not create an instantiation of an attack pattern for every initial step for every employee. We have managed to trim the number of attack pattern instances per employee by updating the state in the attack pattern when someone is repeating previous steps to where he is and by treating effectively the timeout event.

The speed in computation depends on the *update* function which performs two steps for each input log: (1) calculating the target transitions by selecting the transitions satisfying the input log and (2) updating the model concerning the target transitions. In worst case scenario, the target transitions are all the transitions in the detection system, so the complexity of the first step is $O(|T|)$. The second step is the update of the model including the update of state-model, transition-model and history. The time complexity is mainly related to the time required to access the specific tuple in the model. Since the state-model for a user is implemented as an array, the complexity is $O(|S|)$. The transition-model is implemented using a key-value pair and we can access the specific transition using the key in $O(1)$. Finally, to update the alert-history we add the new alert to the object, so the complexity for the alert-history is $O(1)$. Accessing a specific tuple in transition-history and timeout-history is $O(1)$, so the complexity of updating transition-history and timeout-history are same. Therefore, the update complexity for a log is $O(|T|)$, and the evaluation time for a dataset is $O(|T||D|)$, where $|D|$ is the number of logs in the dataset.

The design of the system interfaces considered scalability requirements. For the transition statistics, the records for transitions were grouped and represented by table of records rather than listed plainly, which significantly increased the readability of records. Also, the tool uses D3.js to implement the graphs and charts in the interface. It represents the graphs and charts by DOM manipulation. However, the performance of D3.js degrades significantly as the volume of data increases. In stress-testing datasets with large number of employees (more than 20000), the program ran out of memory. One solution for this is to render the graphs and charts in the back-end and present them in the browser. This could resolve the smoothness problem and the memory issue. However, the interactions would be disabled as the charts are static images.

5   Conclusions

The topic of insider threat has attracted the interested of the research community the last 20 years. A strand of literature has focused on proposing theoretical frameworks to conceptualise the problem whereas a different strand has emphasised on proposing anomaly detection systems. Organisations, in an attempt to mitigate risks from insider threats have developed security policies and rule-based systems to monitor for violations of these policies. In this paper we proposed a state machine system which complements all the aforementioned developments and combines data from detection systems and rule-based systems. Our system enables analysts to design and test attack patterns, incorporate data from anomaly detection or policy violation systems into these patterns and obtain a holistic understanding of the actions that employees perform. We have validated our approach on ten synthetic scenarios and by implementing the attack patterns provided in [3] we were able to detect the perpetrators in seven of these scenarios without generating false positive alerts. We have shown that our system is scalable in terms of computational time and memory usage, since the time complexity depends linearly on the size of the attack patterns and the memory complexity depends linearly on the product of the number of employees and the size of the attack patterns. Finally our system can provide real-time alerts for better situational awareness. Moving forward we intend to improve the performance of our system by adding a multi-threading module and deploy it on a real organisation.

Appendix 1.A   Dataset for Every Scenario

The detection system can have access to both raw data logs and alerts from anomaly detection systems. In our evaluation, these datasets contain both the organisation logs and the alerts generated by the CITD system which is in the same format with the other logs. Logs in each dataset are stored as cmss files, including

- cmss, which are the alerts generated by CITD system,
- cmss, which records the target addresses of emails sent by the users,
- cmss, which records the history of login and logout of the users,
- cmss, which contains the path of files accessed by the users,
- cmss, which records the URLs of websites accessed by the users,
- and cmss, containing the activity related to usb (inserted, removed).

This cmss data is composed by the attributes cmss, cmss, cmss and cmss which refer to the user's id, the time when this log is generated, the device's id and the behaviour of the user recorded by this log. An example of a row in the cmss is:

```
tellis1985,17/05/2013 14:49:11,PC025,http://sourceforge.net
```

Alert logs store the alert information in cmss and the severity of this alert in the extended attribute cmss which can be "Green", "Yellow" and "Red" as explained in [2]. An example of an alert data is:

```
{text}
    dricha1967,01/01/2013 06:39:19,PC060,Out of hours login,Red
```

Files for the same scenario are merged and sorted according to their cmss so we have a file for each scenario containing all the logs from oldest to newest. In addition to the logs, the information of employees and their occupation role duties is also provided for each dataset. This information can be further used in building novel attack patterns or refining current ones. For example, we may want to detect and add a step if any employee accesses sensitive files where admin is part of a path or a name of a file.

Appendix 1.B   Attack Patterns

Figure 8 shows the attack pattern which raised an alert for the scenario explained in detail in Sect. 4. The texts next to the transitions contain the ids of the original attack steps in [3] and brief descriptions of the implementation of the transitions. For example, the transition from S_0 to S_1 in Fig. 8 refers to the attack step cmss that insiders login to the organisations' system using own credentials and this is implemented by capturing the logs in login system with value cmss.

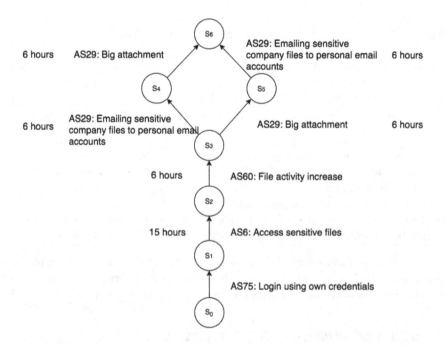

Fig. 8. The attack pattern which generated an alert in our scenario

Figure 9 illustrates the trace followed by the insider (which is highlighted) and the thickness of the arrows in the figure represents the frequency of the transitions.

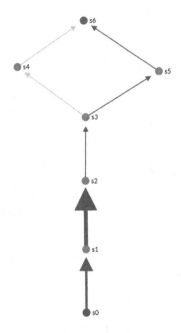

Fig. 9. The attack path which the insider followed in Scenario 1 (Color figure online)

Appendix 1.C   Pattern Editor

Figure 10 presents the pattern editor interface and illustrates how analysts can straightforwardly design novel attack patterns without the need to change the code of the tool.

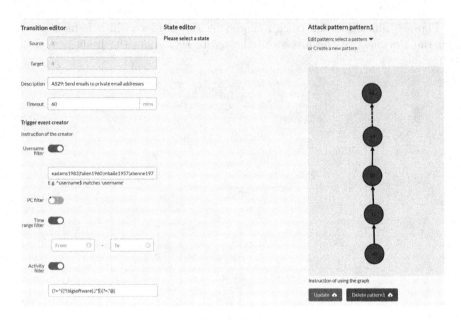

Fig. 10. The interface of the pattern editor

References

1. Agrafiotis, I., Erola, A., Goldsmith, M., Creese, S.: Formalising policies for insider-threat detection: a tripwire grammar. J. Wirel. Mob. Netw. Ubiquit. Comput. Dependable Appl. (JoWUA) **8**(1), 26–43 (2017)
2. Agrafiotis, I., Erola, A., Happa, J., Goldsmith, M., Creese, S.: Validating an insider threat detection system: a real scenario perspective. In: 2016 IEEE Security and Privacy Workshops (SPW), pp. 286–295. IEEE (2016)
3. Agrafiotis, I., Nurse, J.R., Buckley, O., Legg, P., Creese, S., Goldsmith, M.: Identifying attack patterns for insider threat detection. Comput. Fraud Secur. **2015**(7), 9–17 (2015)
4. Arulampalam, M.S., Maskell, S., Gordon, N., Clapp, T.: A tutorial on particle filters for online nonlinear/non-Gaussian Bayesian tracking. IEEE Trans. Sig. Process. **50**(2), 174–188 (2002)
5. Bishop, M., et al.: Insider threat identification by process analysis. In: 2014 IEEE Security and Privacy Workshops (SPW), pp. 251–264. IEEE (2014)
6. Bostock, M.: D3.js. Data Driven Doc. **492**, 701 (2012)
7. Brdiczka, O., et al.: Proactive insider threat detection through graph learning and psychological context. In: 2012 IEEE Symposium on Security and Privacy Workshops (SPW), pp. 142–149. IEEE (2012)
8. Gemalto's Breach Level Index: Data breach database and risk assessment calculator (2016). http://www.breachlevelindex.com/
9. Buford, J.F., Lewis, L., Jakobson, G.: Insider threat detection using situation-aware MAS. In: 2008 11th International Conference on Information Fusion, pp. 1–8. IEEE (2008)

10. Cappelli, D.M., Moore, A.P., Trzeciak, R.F.: The CERT Guide to Insider Threats: How to Prevent, Detect, and Respond to Information Technology Crimes (Theft, Sabotage, Fraud). Addison-Wesley, Boston (2012)
11. Chen, Y., Malin, B.: Detection of anomalous insiders in collaborative environments via relational analysis of access logs. In: Proceedings of the First ACM Conference on Data and Application Security and Privacy, pp. 63–74. ACM (2011)
12. Eberle, W., Graves, J., Holder, L.: Insider threat detection using a graph-based approach. J. Appl. Secur. Res. 6(1), 32–81 (2010)
13. Fedosejev, A.: React.js Essentials. Packt Publishing Ltd., Birmingham (2015)
14. Health Professions Education Unit United Kingdom: Ponemon cyber crime report: it, computer and internet security (2015). http://www8.hp.com/uk/en/software-solutions/ponemon-cyber-security-report/
15. Magklaras, G., Furnell, S.: Insider threat prediction tool: evaluating the probability of IT misuse. Comput. Secur. 21(1), 62–73 (2001)
16. Moore, A.P., Cappelli, D., Caron, T.C., Shaw, E.D., Spooner, D., Trzeciak, R.F.: A preliminary model of insider theft of intellectual property (2011)
17. Moore, A.P., Cappelli, D.M., Trzeciak, R.F.: The "Big Picture" of insider IT sabotage across U.S. critical infrastructures. In: Stolfo, S.J., Bellovin, S.M., Keromytis, A.D., Hershkop, S., Smith, S.W., Sinclair, S. (eds.) Insider Attack and Cyber Security, pp. 17–52. Springer, Heidelberg (2008). https://doi.org/10.1007/978-0-387-77322-3_3
18. Myers, J., Grimaila, M.R., Mills, R.F.: Towards insider threat detection using web server logs. In: Proceedings of the 5th Annual Workshop on Cyber Security and Information Intelligence Research: Cyber Security and Information Intelligence Challenges and Strategies, p. 54. ACM (2009)
19. Nurse, J.R., et al.: Understanding insider threat: a framework for characterising attacks. In: 2014 IEEE Security and Privacy Workshops (SPW), pp. 214–228. IEEE (2014)
20. Nurse, J.R.C., et al.: A critical reflection on the threat from human insiders – its nature, industry perceptions, and detection approaches. In: Tryfonas, T., Askoxylakis, I. (eds.) HAS 2014. LNCS, vol. 8533, pp. 270–281. Springer, Cham (2014). https://doi.org/10.1007/978-3-319-07620-1_24
21. Parveen, P., Thuraisingham, B.: Unsupervised incremental sequence learning for insider threat detection. In: 2012 IEEE International Conference on Intelligence and Security Informatics (ISI), pp. 141–143. IEEE (2012)
22. Rashid, T., Agrafiotis, I., Nurse, J.R.: A new take on detecting insider threats: exploring the use of hidden Markov models. In: Proceedings of the 2016 International Workshop on Managing Insider Security Threats, pp. 47–56. ACM (2016)
23. ISACA and RSA Conference: State of Cybersecurity: implications for 2015 (2015). http://www.isaca.org/cyber/Documents/State-of-Cybersecurity_Res_Eng_0415.pdf
24. Sarkar, K.R.: Assessing insider threats to information security using technical, behavioural and organisational measures. Inf. Secur. Tech. Rep. 15(3), 112–133 (2010)
25. Tilkov, S., Vinoski, S.: Node.js: using Javascript to build high-performance network programs. IEEE Internet Comput. 14(6), 80–83 (2010)
26. Upton, D.M., Creese, S.: The danger from within. Harv. Bus. Rev. 92(9), 94–101 (2014)
27. Young, W.T., Memory, A., Goldberg, H.G., Senator, T.E.: Detecting unknown insider threat scenarios. In: 2014 IEEE Security and Privacy Workshops, pp. 277–288, May 2014. https://doi.org/10.1109/SPW.2014.42

Author Index

Printed in the United States
By Bookmasters